THE LANGUAGE OF SILENCE

TRADITIONS OF CHRISTIAN SPIRITUALITY SERIES

At the Fountain of Elijah: The Carmelite Tradition
Wilfrid McGreal o. carm.

Brides in the Desert: The Spirituality of the Beguines
Saskia Murk-Jansen

Contemplation and Compassion: The Victorine Tradition
Steven Chase

Eyes to See, Ears to Hear: An Introduction to Ignatian Spirituality
David Lonsdale

God's Lovers in an Age of Anxiety: The Medieval English Mystics
Joan M. Nuth

Journeys on the Edges: The Celtic Tradition
Thomas O'Loughlin

Mysticism and Prophecy: The Dominican Tradition
Richard Woods OP

Our Restless Heart: The Augustinian Tradition
Thomas F. Martin OSA

The Poetic Imagination: An Anglican Spiritual Tradition
L. William Countryman

Poverty and Joy: The Franciscan Tradition
William J. Short OFM

Prayer and Community: The Benedictine Tradition
Columba Stewart OSB

Standing in God's Holy Fire: The Byzantine Spiritual Tradition
John Anthony McGuckin

The Spirit of Worship: The Liturgical Tradition
Susan J. White

The Way of Simplicity: The Cistercian Tradition
Esther de Waal

THE LANGUAGE OF SILENCE

The Changing Face of Monastic Solitude

PETER-DAMIAN BELISLE OSB Cam

SERIES EDITOR:
Philip Sheldrake

ORBIS BOOKS
Maryknoll, New York 10545

Founded in 1970, Orbis Books endeavors to publish works that enlighten the mind, nourish the spirit, and challenge the conscience. The publishing arm of the Maryknoll Fathers & Brothers, Orbis seeks to explore the global dimensions of the Christian faith and mission, to invite dialogue with diverse cultures and religious traditions, and to serve the cause of reconciliation and peace. The books published reflect the views of their authors and do not represent the official position of the Society. To learn more about Maryknoll and Orbis Books, please visit our website at www.maryknoll.org.

First published in Great Britain in 2003 by
Darton, Longman and Todd Ltd
1 Spencer Court
140–142 Wandsworth High Street
London SW18 4JJ
Great Britain

First published in the USA in 2003 by
Orbis Books
P.O. Box 308
Maryknoll, New York 10545–0308
U.S.A.

Printed and bound in Great Britain.

Library of Congress Cataloging-in-Publication Data

Belisle, Peter-Damian, 1947–
    The language of silence : the changing face of monastic solitude / Peter-Damian Belisle.
        p.   cm.—(Traditions of Christian spirituality series)
Includes bibliographical references (p.   ).
    ISBN 1–57075–486–1 (pbk.)
    1. Hermits. 2. Solitude—Religious aspects—Christianity—History of Doctrines. 3. Solitude—Religious aspects—Catholic Church—History of Doctrines. I. Title. II. Traditions of Christian spirituality.
BX2845 .B45 2003
248.4′7—dc21   2003010483

Dedicated

to my sister Barb –
a lovely, loving woman

CONTENTS

ACKNOWLEDGEMENTS

Permission is granted by the Order of St Benedict to reprint here a portion of the chapter 'Golden Solitude' from *The Privilege of Love: Camaldolese Benedictine Spirituality*, published by The Liturgical Press, Collegeville, Minnesota, 2002.

I am particularly grateful to the following individuals:
Columba Stewart OSB for his initial suggestion that I research the topic of monastic solitude;
Paulette Boudreaux and my confrères Romuald Duscher OSB Cam and Isaiah Teichert OSB Cam for their generosity in proofreading the manuscript;
Robert Hale OSB Cam for his timely referral;
Philip Sheldrake and Robert Ellsberg for their helpful suggestions regarding Part Four of the book.

PREFACE TO THE SERIES

Nowadays, in the western world, there is a widespread hunger for spirituality in all its forms. This is not confined to traditional religious people let alone to regular churchgoers. The desire for resources to sustain the spiritual quest has led many people to seek wisdom in unfamiliar places. Some have turned to cultures other than their own. The fascination with Native American or Aboriginal Australian spiritualities is a case in point. Other people have been attracted by the religions of India and Tibet or the Jewish Kabbalah and Sufi mysticism. One problem is that, in comparison to other religions, Christianity is not always associated in people's minds with 'spirituality'. The exceptions are a few figures from the past who have achieved almost cult status such as Hildegard of Bingen or Meister Eckhart. This is a great pity, for Christianity East and West over two thousand years has given birth to an immense range of spiritual wisdom. Many traditions continue to be active today. Others that were forgotten are being rediscovered and reinterpreted.

It is a long time since an extended series of introductions to Christian spiritual traditions has been available in English. Given the present climate, it is an opportune moment for a new series which will help more people to be aware of the great spiritual riches available within the Christian tradition.

The overall purpose of the series is to make selected spiritual traditions available to a contemporary readership. The books seek to provide accurate and balanced historical and thematic treatments of their subjects. The authors are also conscious of the need to make connections with contemporary experience and values without being artificial or reducing a tradition to one dimension. The authors are well versed in reliable scholarship about the traditions they describe. However, their intention is that the books should be fresh in style and accessible to the general reader.

One problem that such a series inevitably faces is the word 'spirituality'. For example, it is increasingly used beyond religious circles and does not necessarily imply a faith tradition. Again, it could mean substantially different things for a Christian and a Buddhist. Within Christianity itself, the word in its modern sense is relatively recent. The reality that it stands for differs subtly in the different contexts of time and place. Historically, 'spirituality' covers a breadth of human experience and a wide range of values and practices.

No single definition of 'spirituality' has been imposed on the authors in this series. Yet, despite the breadth of the series there is a sense of a common core in the writers themselves and in the traditions they describe. All Christian spiritual traditions have their source in three things. First, while drawing on ordinary experience and even religious insights from elsewhere, Christian spiritualities are rooted in the Scriptures and particularly in the Gospels. Second, spiritual traditions are not derived from abstract theory but from attempts to live out gospel values in a positive yet critical way within specific historical and cultural contexts. Third, the experiences and insights of individuals and groups are not isolated but are related to the wider Christian tradition of beliefs, practices and community life. From a Christian perspective, spirituality is not just concerned with prayer or even with narrowly religious activities. It concerns the whole of human life, viewed in terms of a conscious relationship with God, in Jesus Christ, through the indwelling of the Holy Spirit and within a community of believers.

The series as a whole includes traditions that probably would not have appeared twenty years ago. The authors themselves have been encouraged to challenge, where appropriate, inaccurate assumptions about their particular tradition. While conscious of their own biases, authors have none the less sought to correct the imbalances of the past. Previous understandings of what is mainstream or 'orthodox' sometimes need to be questioned. People or practices that became marginal demand to be re-examined. Studies of spirituality in the past frequently underestimated or ignored the role of women. Sometimes the treatments of spiritual traditions were culturally one-sided because they were written from an uncritical Western European or North Atlantic perspective.

However, any series is necessarily selective. It cannot hope to do full justice to the extraordinary variety of Christian spiritual traditions. The principles of selection are inevitably open to question. I hope that an appropriate balance has been maintained between a sense of the likely readership on the one hand and the dangers of narrowness on the other. In the end, choices had to be made and the result is inevitably weighted in favour of traditions that have achieved 'classic' status or which seem to capture the contemporary imagination. Within these limits, I trust that the series will offer a reasonably balanced account of what the Christian spiritual tradition has to offer.

As editor of the series I would like to thank all the authors who agreed to contribute and for the stimulating conversations and correspondence that sometimes resulted. I am especially grateful for the high quality of their work which made my task so much easier. Editing such a series is a complex undertaking. I have worked closely throughout with the editorial team of Darton, Longman and Todd and Robert Ellsberg of Orbis Books. I am immensely grateful to them for their friendly support and judicious advice. Without them this series would never have come together.

PHILIP SHELDRAKE
Sarum College, Salisbury

1. INTRODUCTION: THE SILENT COMMUNION OF SOLITUDE

Being alone in silence can be a terrifying experience for one adverse to introspection or fearful of loneliness, but aloneness and quiet will be welcome solace and even pleasure for others. The shades of solitude cover motivation's spectrum from the rare light of eremitical ecstasy to the darkest hues of isolated misanthropy. From the adolescent's solitude brooding over metaphysics to an elder's quiet solitude coming to terms with death, we all experience various kinds of solitude during a lifetime. We find ourselves surrounded by life's paradoxes, and we try to come to grips with the seeming absurdities of existence to approach the mystery of truth whose germ is present at the pith of paradox. Those of us who are 'seized' by life's paradoxes tend to devote ourselves to the truth within these contrasts, knowing we must place ourselves in the midst of the oppositions. We must be at the centre of reality and sustain that centredness for any real continuity. When we grasp truth within paradox, we transcend its conflict of oppositions and apprehend meaning. In the context of religious consciousness, we encounter God's presence and discover new meaning through a relationship with that presence.

Every human person is unique; every human heart is unique. To the extent that a person's interiority has fostered self-knowledge and personal integrity, solitude itself can help cultivate creativity. We can think of poets, painters, sculptors and potters as the truly unique individuals, but of course, we are all really unique. The artists simply have more facility for communicating their unique inner world through creative intuition and artistic inspiration. They are those who have revealed their innermost secrets to the world. They have taken their uniqueness and given it shape.[1] Each one of us has a unique inner core to explore and express. Solitude enables and encourages us to encounter that deeply personal mystery.

Indeed, we all need solitude in order to achieve some modicum of personal integrity. There are times for the company of others; there are times to be alone. We humans need our solitude as much as we need our community.[2] Being alone allows the heart to awaken and, if one embraces that experience of solitude, the possibility for personal growth is enhanced. Solitude is not loneliness. When a person turns inward to solitude, that movement is away from loneliness and into aloneness. What is the difference? Presence is there, and encounter. Solitude is necessary for personal growth.[3]

Unafraid of inner suffering, the awakened heart will even take comfort in solitude. Solitude is solidarity with one's own being; it is oneness as well as aloneness.[4] The religious person seeks solitude in order to seek God, to listen to and speak with God. Being alone allows the readied heart to encounter God. It is not good simply to flee society in order to get away from all people. True solitude has a positive movement about it – a search for meaning and presence, for God.[5] One is never alone in true solitude. There is the powerful experience of presence that rises out of solitude's depths, much like the experience of finding a 'soulmate' in a new relationship. It is as though solitude really brings about a face-to-face, heart-to-heart encounter at the innermost depths of the solitary.[6]

During the early centuries of church history, men and women departed for desert wastelands from the towns and cities of Egypt, Palestine and Syria, to find God in solitude and to fight battles with demons standing in the way of relationship with God. Here was an intensification of the search for God in a desert without all the diversions and escapes so readily available in the towns. At certain periods, loose settlements of desert solitaries grew so large that the more fervent seekers once again felt the need to pick up stakes and move even further afield in the wilderness. Separation is meant to encourage union with God, if prayer and ascetical effort are present. One really needs solitude of some sort to provide an opportunity for contemplative union. Asceticism helps both to prepare the mind and to condition the body to focus on encounter.[7] Over the centuries, the call to the 'inner' desert has demanded the same separation/solitude, prayer and asceticism of men and women seeking God in monastic intensity.

The monastic heart has entered the inner desert in hermitages, cenobitic monasteries, lauras or groupings of hermitages, forests, mountains, caves, deserts, secluded valleys and remote islands. Separation and solitude have provided, encouraged and nurtured access to that inner desert. The solace found by contemporary monastics does not derive merely from the absence of guests or the ever-present – and sometimes, noisy – demands of community life. The separation of the cell seems a necessary means to the inner desert. A monk or nun finds respite in the cell that allows them to keep their equilibrium. This is perhaps more true today than ever in monasteries. The equilibrium finds a working balance between word and silence, solitude and community.[8]

The monastic seeker who discovers there is no more time for the inner work runs a perilous course because one's outer life so depends upon the inner life. True solitude helps a person to come face to face with that unique inner world at their centre, to come to know and accept its value, to find the strength to love that uniqueness in God's presence, and to live it in communion with others. 'Here is a call to honest aloneness where one is really not alone at all, but awake to God's presence. For solitude entices us into Presence.'[9] The encounter with Presence in the space provided by solitude can and should become a transformative encounter within that liminal space. We stand utterly naked in all our uniqueness in God's presence. And our encounter with Mystery will touch us with healing, *penthos* (deep compunction), gratitude and challenge in ways unthinkable elsewhere. For the inner desert truly is a liminal place where we run the great risk of transformation into our unique selves, more fully who we are meant to be, in the grace of personal integration. To enter the inner desert is one thing, but to be there regularly with open authenticity is quite another. 'Standing at the prophetic margin can require patient determination, but allowing that margin to become a threshold for the encounter between meaning and mystery will demand courage and perseverance.'[10]

How does one gauge the efficacy of solitude? How is true solitude different from an exercise in isolation or a lonely ego trip? The fruit of authentic solitude is communion. If one enters solitude only in order to escape people or noise, that is not enough! One is never really alone in solitude. Encountering God's presence protects the solitary from an ego-centred shallowness.[11] Communion with God in solitude extends itself to communion with others. Someone who is comfortable with the self and being alone in the presence of God will also be comfortable with others in that presence. Solitude can bring depth and enhancement to relationships.[12]

Solitude moves towards communion. I am in solitude to experience a presence and I move out of solitude to share that experience with others. Solitude, at its most authentic, moves from communion to communion. This kind of communion forms community at a powerfully intuitive level because bonding within the framework of communion implies profound commonality. Communion is a compenetration of being at a moment always 'now' and in a manner ever 'present'.

Silence is the language spoken by solitude. Perhaps at first reckoning, we might consider silence merely the absence of sound. But silence is not something that begins only when sound ends. There is something awesome and breathtaking about real silence; it is numinous, pulling us out of our self-containment and calling us towards the invisible. Religious seekers 'home in' on silence as homing pigeons return to their roost, because therein lies the language for personal communication with the sacred.

Referring to Picard and Sciacca's works on the philosophy of solitude, Ambrose Wathen affirms how silence gives birth and meaning to every word. Silence is the origin of speech.[13] Picard himself uses the image of pregnancy in reference to speech coming out of silence, as a child comes forth from a pregnant mother.[14] The Spirit becomes a midwife who helps bring the word out of the silence. In this same context, Jean Leclercq points out that our silence within us liberates the word.[15] It is an active part of speech, not simply the lack of sound within it. Silence helps us all to discover who we really are, and in so doing, participates in the sacramentality of personhood. Silence accompanies us into our innermost selves where we are present to the sacred. When word breaks into that kind of silence, there is communion.[16]

There are both inner silence (taciturnity) and outer, physical silence. And due to the nature of this book, I will no doubt weave my way between these two realities that can be further distinguished by psychological motivations (e.g. angry, hateful silence) and external circumstances (e.g. penal isolation). We should not view speech in opposition to silence, as if words were inimical to the reality engendering them. Monastics have always tried, at least in theory, to curb the flow of words in order to enhance the presence and power of silence. They do so out of respect for the power of the word – and the Word. Writing of the monastic spiritual leaders in nineteenth-century Russia who maintained their inner silence (*hesychia*) while communicating with visitors, Kallistos Ware describes how their words to each visitor were powerful words precisely because silence lay beneath them.[17]

People are finding less silence in today's societies. They seek out places of refuge and retreat, hoping for the blessing of mere quiet and perhaps, sheer silence. They go to monasteries and hermitages so they can learn to listen, or listen more attentively. Within monastic walls, silence is maintained so as not to disturb anyone who may be listening to the Word or simply resting the body.[18] But listening is crucial there, and people recognise that fact instinctively. To what are monastics listening in their silence? To the word of God; to their innermost hearts; to grace at work in the spirit; to what they discern to be truth – ultimate truth. Here is the place where one is ultimately completely naked – stripped of all pretension and illusion – and where one stands truly as one is in the presence of God.[19] Here one stands, simply and utterly, in truth.

This kind of silence – that deepest, innermost kind – reveals itself in so many ways. And each revelation carries within a potential moment of awakening, a further elaboration of the mystery calling us to be there in a fuller fashion. With each new revelation awakened and envisioned, we come to know ourselves better as we truly are and catch yet another glimpse of ourselves in relationship with God, as mystery reaches out to Mystery. The more often we can authentically enter this transformative silence, the better our chances to become who we are meant to be in God's presence. This silence is an awakening of our deepest yearnings and aspirations.

In silence we commune with God's presence, the fullest manifestation of love in our experience; indeed, here is love itself. And the language of silence is a language of love because love is so near God's presence. In love the silence of God became the Word of God for humanity. The more we speak the language of love, the more consciously we embrace that Word. And love resonates clearly in that deep silence that gave it birth. Each of us first meets God in silence, but the word spoken at that meeting will be unique.[20]

People who choose a monastic manner of life do so, in part, for ready, conscious recourse to God's presence in silence, where their thirst for God is never fully quenched, but even increased. The language of love articulates our prayer to God. Our words come out of silence and pierce through that deeper silence of God's presence. Our words are never enough, always inadequate to express fully our deepest longings. The tradition of Christian monastic prayer has long held that the purest prayer lies in maintaining an inner silence before that greater silence. Monastics try to keep an inner silence perduring, even when surrounded by the myriad noises of twenty-first-century life. Then, whenever possible, they enter the silence to intensify their language of love.

Silence is the seedbed for spiritual growth and maturity wherein a person lays bare the heart, without pretence or deception. The monastic aim is to live all of life with a transparency exposing the heart to all, as the Gospel would have it. Monks and nuns learn to approach all reality in anticipation of an encounter with mystery. Silence allows that to happen, providing an awareness (mindfulness) of sacred presence. And silence nurtures vigilance and waiting for communion.[21] Silence is a locus of surrender for a life of surrender. And in self-surrender, monastics embrace the world around them as an icon of love.

Because silence is a locus of surrender, it is a way to union and communion. We have only to think of Jesus in the garden of Gethsemani or on the gibbet of the cross to see the necessity for silence in spiritual growth. Silence is, thus, a monastic absolute. Monastics enter solitude to be united to all in silent communion. Far from being misanthropic escapes from the world, true monastic solitude and silence are precious gifts to the world and for the world. The only way for the heart of humanity to be truly universal is to come into union with universal love. The monastic heart strives to embrace that very union in the silent communion of solitude.

PART ONE: DESERT ROOTS

2. FIGURES OF OLD TESTAMENT SOLITUDE

Before investigating the phenomenon of solitude in the early Christian deserts, we should treat, if only cursorily, some of the biblical figures of both Testaments whom these early Christian desert solitaries (and indeed, monastics throughout the centuries) were to typify in their oral and written traditions as models of solitude. Both Moses and Elijah came to represent solitude in the wilderness, in communion with God's presence in different ways. Though the Song of Songs appears less than Moses and Elijah, admittedly, this love poem does appear in reference to the desert *ammas* (mothers) and *abbas* (fathers). And among the medieval Cistercian writers especially, the Song of Songs became a favourite source for discourses on the inner desert, union, communion and mystical marriage. The desert is a place of physical solitude, austere simplicity, stark beauty and dire danger. It is a place for inner battles, visions and dreams, encounters, and perhaps theophanies.

MOSES

Surely one of the most solitary figures in biblical literature, by anyone's reckoning, is Moses. From his infancy floating among the Nile reeds to the final glimpse of him atop Mount Nebo, Moses was starkly alone. Evidently, Moses felt drawn regularly into solitude by natural propensity. The biographical data at hand portrays a man quite comfortable with being alone. Although historical circumstances often cornered him into a solitary stance, still, Moses was there also by choice at pivotal points in his life. Moses seemed to have been at his best in solitude.[1] Much of his later life seems to have been spent climbing up into theophanous light and climbing back down to deal with the inevitable problems of the Jews he was leading through desert wastes towards the Promised Land. As Divo Barsotti notes, Moses' entire journey is a climb.[2]

After Moses had fled from Egypt to the desert of Midian, married a non-Jewess and lived as a shepherd with her family, he was alone with his flock one day at Mount Sinai (variously, Horeb) and noticed flame coming from an acacia bush that remained unscorched by the fire. Why was he on Sinai? To find his flock? To locate good grazing for the sheep? Maybe he went there for some solitude! Out of that bush sounded God's voice calling him by name. In one sense, Moses was no longer alone in God's presence, but as Wiesel points out, Moses is more alone than ever because it is just he and God.[3] God told Moses to remove his sandals out of respect for the sacredness of the event. Once he realised it was the God of his ancestors speaking to him from the burning bush, Moses shielded himself from the view.

Commissioned by God to return to Egypt, gather the Jews and lead them out of Egypt to the Promised Land, Moses was stunned by the order and tried his best to sidestep it by claiming the Jews would not listen to him; besides, he was not a public speaker. But God gave Moses a new name for God, the power to change his staff into a serpent, to heal leprosy, and to change the Nile River into blood. Moses still tried to wriggle his way out of the mission, but even though he brought Aaron into the picture, Moses could not escape God's command.[4] And so, Aaron became Moses' spokesman, while Moses himself remained God's spokesman. He returned to the desert, and then to Egypt to fulfil his commission received in solitude, in his face-to-face encounter with God.

Once Moses had wrested the Jews from Egypt's grip and led them through the desert to the foot of Mount Sinai, the prophet again found himself climbing the mountain in solitude to encounter Yahweh, the God of his ancestors. His role as intermediary between God and the Jews quickened pace as Moses ascended and descended Sinai, ironing out a covenant. Later interpretations of exactly what happened during this period and interpolations of various sets of laws have produced a somewhat confusing account of events in Exodus 19—20, 24, 32—34. Although Moses seems to have been quite busy climbing up and down Sinai, he likely only did so a few times.

Moses' propensity to spend time in solitude atop Mount Sinai for long periods while the restless people waited below in uncertainty and boredom is not simply a colourful anecdote. As with the burning bush episode, Moses was once again drawn to solitary meditation. We are told Moses' face shone so brightly from his divine encounters that he had to veil himself whenever dealing with the people. Even when back among the people, Moses had to separate himself from them. From the outset, Moses' relationship with the Jews followed a rocky road, but despite their stubbornness and grumbling on the one hand and his harsh reaction to their fickleness and infidelity on the other, Moses' personal tenacity and devotion held true to the end. Moses lived a strong faith in God, but his undying love for and devotion to God's people were just as strong.[5]

But as Elie Wiesel points out, Moses is still the loneliest man in the Old Testament.[6] His task seems almost impossible, especially if he was introverted by nature. How he got through it all and brought a more cohesive people to the threshold of their destination must have owed its success to Moses' solitary relationship with God. But solitude exacts a price. He spent so much time in the 'tent of meeting' in the desert, he seems to have missed much of the life of the people, as he prayed, pondered and meditated in solitude. But once many of the organisational problems were solved and the people a cohesive, reasonably functioning entity, they could turn towards the Promised Land.

After scouting out the land of Canaan that God had designated as that land promised to Abraham, Isaac and Jacob, the people of Israel defeated King Sihon, King Og and the kings of Midian. But Moses did not cross the Jordan and enter the Promised Land with his people. Instead, God called him to yet another mountain summit – Pisgah on Mount Nebo. There he saw the Promised Land he would not enter as he stood in solitude at his life's end. Surely, this was his most solitary moment. Martin Buber described this sad vignette from the prophet's life as reminiscent of animals that wander off to die alone away from the rest of the group.[7] This most solitary of prophets ended his life of public service to his people in the same way he began it – on top of a mountain in solitude.

ELIJAH

A few centuries later, another prophet-patriarch blazed onto the scene of Israel's history during the reign of King Ahab, whose father Omri had arranged his marriage to the Phoenician princess Jezebel, a strong and dominant personality devoted to the worship of Baal and Asherah. Elijah the Tishbite from Gilead rose up to champion the God of Israel whose prophets Jezebel had tried to exterminate. The Book of Sirach would later refer to Elijah as 'fire' (cf. Sir. 48:1) whose word shone like a torch. Fire is an apt image for Elijah whose sacrifice on Mount Carmel was consumed by heavenly fire; who witnessed, as Moses did before him, fire at Sinai's (Horeb's) summit; and who ascended to heaven in a fiery chariot within a blink of an eye for Elisha – Elijah's prophetic successor. Elijah is the prophet of fire.

He is a second Moses who has his own desert experience and whose word brings drought and famine upon the land, just like Moses in Egypt. Elijah made his way to Sinai where he, like Moses, experienced intimately God's presence and personal revelation. And like Moses, God commissioned Elijah to work for the covenant in Israel. Because the transfiguration of Jesus as told in the New Testament would imprint so strongly in the imaginations of the first monastics in the desert tradition, both Moses and Elijah entered significantly into monastic consciousness. Like Moses, Elijah was another figure of deep solitude. Suddenly he appeared alone to announce a drought for Israel, during which he mostly lived alone in the wilderness of Cherith on water from the wadi and food provided by ravens. Even though there had been many prophets in Israel prior to Jezebel's arrival, Elijah appeared to have been on his own, solitary. Even when instructed on Mount Sinai to anoint Elisha his successor, Elijah keeps him at a distance. Only in his last moments does Elijah lessen the distance between them. He enjoyed in his solitude a personal intimacy with God that sustained him (quite literally at times), and then propelled him towards further prophetic actions. As with Moses, Elie Wiesel remarks upon Elijah's total aloneness.[8] Even when people were around, Elijah was alone.

But Elijah was not always in solitude. His periods of stark solitude are followed by intense periods of prophetic activity on behalf of God and the people. His life pattern could be seen as a seesaw of solitary contemplation and furious action. True, he only broke his solitude whenever God told him to do so, but he did so unhesitatingly. Elijah left his hiding place near the Wadi Cherith to assist the widow of Zarephath and her son. He prevailed over the Baal prophets on Mount Carmel and regained the people for the God of Israel. He anointed Elisha as his successor, who then became his disciple until Elijah's final departure. Elijah predicted the deaths of Ahab, Jezebel and Ahaziah. Whenever he broke solitude, Elijah did so for the sake of his people and their covenant with the God of Israel. The early desert monastics were most drawn to the prophet Elijah's penchant for solitude. Elijah was their hero and desert forebear. They saw him remain in solitude at Cherith; battle alone against the forces of idolatry; journey alone through the desert to Sinai, that place of theophany; ascend to heaven in a blaze of fire; and appear with Moses at the side of the transfigured Christ on Mount Tabor.

When Elijah suddenly appeared before King Ahab and proclaimed a three-year drought in the name of the Lord, the prophet heard God telling him to go east of the Jordan River and hide by the Wadi Cherith. He was there a long time, waiting on God, for God directed Elijah in and out of his solitude for the remainder of his life. At the famous encounter between Elijah and the prophets of Baal on Mount Carmel, the prophet was strikingly alone – pitted against the opposition and outside the people's support. But he was fierce and stubbornly uncompromising in his defence of the God of Israel, as well as in his attack on the idolatrous forces of Jezebel and her Baals. Elijah's unwavering stance in the face of all odds would later appeal to the early Christian desert monastics who viewed themselves as God's warriors, like this fiery prophet. The bloody outcome on Carmel did nothing to endear Elijah to the political powers, but the mass execution of the Baal prophets could not help but impress upon the memories of those gathered there the proof of God's power and presence in the holocaustal sacrifice. Elijah was not trying to gain popularity with the people, but to win them back to God. As far as popularity was concerned, once he heard Jezebel's intent to kill him, Elijah fled for his life!

Elijah turned again to solitude in the desert. Not only was he physically in flight, but judging by his desire to die (1 Kings 19:4), Elijah was also in psychological panic and spiritual despair. Once again, God intervened with sustenance and encouraged the prophet to continue his flight. Slowly Elijah made his way to Mount Sinai. Four centuries earlier, Moses had experienced his theophanies on Mount Sinai; now Elijah followed suit. He spent the night in a cave. The next day, the prophet was unable to discern God's presence in the windstorm, the earthquake and ensuing fire. But Elijah found God in a tiny whispering sound and, like Moses before him, the prophet hid his face in his mantle. God gave him yet more tasks to accomplish.

When Elijah started out on his final journey, he tried to prevent Elisha from accompanying him. But the latter prophet was not about to give way to Elijah's request for solitude, regardless of his motivation. Suddenly, in a flash, a fiery chariot lifted Elijah into the heavens. Like his remarkable life, Elijah's ascension into the heavens was unique and overwhelming. For the early Christian desert-dwellers, the prophet Elijah would return at Christ's transfiguration on Mount

Tabor. So they turned to Elijah, their desert forebear, to find their prototype of how to stand before Christ transfigured.

THE SONG OF SONGS

The poetry of the Song of Songs (Song of Solomon, Canticle of Canticles) has captured the monastic, mystic heart from the earliest Christian centuries. For such a small work – 117 verses – this Old Testament book has kicked up more than its proportionate share of controversial dust! From the outset, both Jewish and Christian commentators have found practically everything about the book questionable, even its authorship, date of composition and literary form. Regarding its meaning, sexual love is clear at the literal level. But where one goes from there has provided a 'farmers' market' of interpretations over the years. For medieval Christianity, the Song of Songs became the most commented upon book of Scripture.[9]

But the medieval monastics followed a long line of commentators, among whose number were such luminaries as Origen, Gregory of Nyssa, Jerome, Augustine, Theodoret of Cyr and Gregory the Great. My purpose here is not to discuss all the various commentaries, but to point out that medieval monastic commentators enjoyed many literary antecedents from whom they derived allegorical meanings and applications. Most Jewish commentators perceived in the Song an allegory of love between God and Israel. Origen replaced Israel with the Church. Later Christian commentators followed Origen's lead, except for a few individuals like Theodore of Mopsuestia who suggested the Song was simply a secular love poem. The fifth Council of Constantinople posthumously condemned Theodore for his opinion. The medieval period engendered both scholastic and monastic commentaries. The former are interested in doctrine and the intellect; the latter are concerned with God in relation to each soul and union. By its nature, poetry lends itself to interpretation. The monastic commentators were eager to plumb the depths of the Song and bring to the surface all the meanings hidden deeply within the text. Gregory the

Great, who himself was indebted to Origen's commentary, was the most important source for later medieval commentators.

But perhaps the themes of seeking and finding that weave throughout the Song are what most captured the hearts of monastic commentators – both Gregory the Great and later monks. Such a theme goes to the heart of the monastic quest. The poem about the lover seeking the beloved – and vice versa – finds a sympathetic ear in the monastery where the life is one of seeking God.[10] What more appropriate vehicle to contemplation for monastics seeking God's presence and striving towards union with God than a poetic dialogue of love? The medieval commentary on the Song of Songs as a dialogue of love and union between God and the soul found its ideal footing among the Cistercian monks of the twelfth century.

The Cistercian reform movement of the Benedictine tradition aimed to recapture the primitive spirit of the *Rule of St Benedict* and grew at a phenomenal rate. Clearly its quintessential spokesman, and at times controversial apologist, was Abbot Bernard of Clairvaux. He wrote many works, among which are his 86 sermons on the Song of Songs delivered and polished during an 18-year period (1135–53), and disseminated quickly throughout the Cistercian family (already numbering hundreds of foundations), as well as among other monastic orders and the general public. Bernard's moral treatment of the Song did not move past chapter 2 by the time he died, so another Cistercian, Gilbert of Hoyland, continued the work with 48 additional sermons, bringing the Cistercian effort to midway through chapter 4. Yet another Cistercian, John of Ford, rose to the challenge and finished off the Cistercian 'Bernardine' treatment of the Song of Songs with another 46 sermons. Although there were other Cistercian commentaries among the many other medieval monastic treatises, only one other stands out with distinction – that of William of St-Thierry, written concurrently with Bernard's series of sermons. William was a good friend of Bernard's and another shining light of medieval Cistercian Benedictine scholarship and mysticism. All of these monks were concerned with the union of God and the soul in the milieu of silence and solitude.

Bernard's collected *Sermons on the Song of Songs* was one of the true masterpieces of the twelfth century, read by communities and individuals seeking monastic and mystical spirituality. The body of work was not intended as biblical exegesis, but as an ongoing *lectio* (reading) meant to move hearts towards contemplative union with God. It would be easy for Bernard to describe the theme of his *Sermons* in one word: love.[11] Some critics have said that the entire Bernardine corpus is ultimately about love. Others have seen little love in Bernard or his works. Instead of mystical love, they read Bernard's personal turmoil and problems with carnality.[12] True, Bernard was single-minded and, when writing, nothing got in the way of his focus on God. For all his personal failings, glimpsed for example in his personal 'crusade' fervour and the vindictiveness with which he pursued Abelard, Bernard's amazing gifts and achievements are undeniable. His *Sermons*, without doubt, constitute one of the most important Latin works of the Middle Ages, and influenced the development of Christian spirituality for centuries.[13] Bernard spoke to all God-seekers to teach them how to seek and to know that they themselves were being sought.[14] But in so doing, Bernard was busy finding himself.[15]

An amazing man in his own right, Abbot Gilbert of Hoyland took up the task of Bernard's project on the Song when the latter died across the Channel. Like Bernard, Gilbert used the Song of Songs to investigate the union of the individual soul with God, and the Church with Christ. John of Ford finished the task. But perhaps the most stunning of the Cistercian efforts was that of William of St-Thierry, Bernard's friend, who collaborated with him on the project from a distance and who concurrently wrote his own treatise. As with his other theological works, William's treatise was very much his own creation, though mentored by Bernard. This was lived *lectio divina* (sacred reading).[16]

3. FIGURES OF NEW TESTAMENT SOLITUDE

Early Christian monastics also found New Testament figures that served as models or types for the monastic lifestyle they had chosen. The three most prominent models for these early Christian desert-dwellers, and indeed for monastics throughout the centuries, were John the Baptist, Jesus Christ and Mary, the Mother of Jesus. From Christian monasticism's inception, John the Baptist served as its prototype: living in the desert wilderness; ministering as prophet; suffering his solitary prison martyrdom. Jesus himself spoke to the life experience of monastics: undergoing temptations in the desert wilderness; seeking prayer in solitude on mountaintops; being transfigured on Mount Tabor. The Virgin Mary also showed monastics how to be true disciples: pregnant with the Word; pondering silently within her heart; suffering with Christ beneath the cross on Golgotha. These three gospel figures have guided monks and nuns into the heart of the monastic ethos, down to the present day. They form the quiet centre of that ever-evolving living iconostasis of praise and adoration that monastic life continually tries to become.

JOHN THE BAPTIST

Monastics have traditionally considered John the Baptist their desert ancestor, a monastic saint, if you will. They see in him a monastic prototype: one who entered the desert and faced the trials of life in the wilderness; who left family and home for a place where he could encounter silence and solitude; who moved to that biblical place of preparation and purification where he could devote himself to fasting, penance and prayer. John lived a unique life and yet, at least for a while, people felt drawn to this 'howling voice in the wilderness'. They found a dishevelled, unkempt man dressed in skins and eating insects, calling them all to repentance and preparation for messianic times. He was the last in a long line of prophets. He saw himself standing at the end of time, on the threshold of the messianic age.[1]

John is mentioned in the New Testament some ninety times, less than only Jesus himself and the apostles Peter and Paul. Because he was the precursor of the Lord, the early Church celebrated John as they did Jesus. Patristic writers considered John's excitement in Elizabeth's womb at the visitation of Mary a sign of his holiness and dedication to Jesus from that moment. John is the only saint, besides the Virgin Mary, whose birth finds liturgical celebration (June 24). Some local churches also celebrated John's conception on September 24. Traditionally, the Church celebrated three masses on June 24 to mirror the Christmas masses celebrating Jesus' birth: a midnight mass to celebrate John the precursor; a dawn mass to celebrate his baptism; and a mass during the day to celebrate his holiness. Jesus himself esteemed John the greatest prophet (Matt. 11:7–11) whose life and martyrdom marked the beginning of the 'New Dispensation' – a hinge between the old and the new.

Mark's gospel account opens with the image of John in the wilderness, proclaiming his baptism of repentance. The Lucan account refers to the Baptist's miraculous conception, birth and circumcision. The child grew and strengthened in spirit and then he was in the desert wilderness (Luke 1:80). It is possible that John was somehow connected with the monastic community of Qumran there in the Judaean desert, but even if not a member or associate of this group that had broken away from Jerusalem Temple worship, he surely knew of their life and their apocalyptic message – much like his own message. Qumran was located in the area near the Dead Sea's northern shore. These Essenes were concerned with ritual purity, bathing, ablutions and baptism. They fasted and enjoyed a simple diet – including locusts and honey, interest-ingly. They saw themselves as an army of light meant to usher in that apocalyptic time of imminent judgement.

John preached his message of repentance and baptised people who flocked to him. They were excited by his intensity and the possibility of messianic times. They considered John a prophet, maybe even Elijah returned to earth. His desert manners appealed to them. Life in the wilderness had con-ditioned him to listen for God in the silence. Some became followers who formed a baptist movement, still extant after John's death. They not only practised John's ritual baptism, but also helped spread his apocalyptic message of preparation for the end-time by fasting, repentance, calling for justice and sharing with those in need. John was certainly a prophet, very much like the single-minded Elijah before him. Both lived in desert wastes, in solitude and silence. Both prophets wore skins and subsisted on desert fare. Both exerted public force against political leaders. Powerful women attached to those same leaders – Jezebel to King Ahaz and Herodias to King Herod – persecuted both. From John's very conception, the angel appearing to Zechariah likened the Baptist to Elijah. People throughout Judaea saw him as Elijah reappearing. Jesus himself made this same connection. John – the voice crying out in the wilderness – prepared the way for Jesus. He had a twofold role: preparing for and pointing out Jesus as the Lamb of God. Once these tasks were accomplished, John faded from the scene as Jesus' public life began. When we next hear of John in any significant way, the Baptist is imprisoned. He had publicly challenged Herod's relationship with Herodias. Once he had been incarcerated at the Machaeus palace on the shore of the Dead Sea, opposite Qumran, Herodias schemed to have the Baptist eliminated. In a rather unsettling scene, John sends his disciples to ask Jesus if he were really the Messiah, after all. He felt bewildered by how the messianic age was taking shape. They beheaded John in his prison soli-tude where he had languished for some time. The 'voice' had been silenced, but the Word was proclaiming throughout Galilee.

Early Christian monastics studying the gospel texts found in John the Baptist a model for the life they themselves aimed to fashion in their own deserts. Patristic writers celebrated in John the prototype for the monastic life. John Cassian wrote of those desert monks who were not afraid to imitate John the Baptist and move into the deepest desert wastes to spend their lives there.[2] Jerome championed John as proto-monk.[3] The medieval Cistercians used John as an example for living the prophetic dimensions of solitary and monastic life. Peter Damian harkened to the penitential dimension of the Baptist while setting down the customary of his own Avellanita Congregation. Bruno dedicated the church of his first Carthusian house in Italy to John the Baptist; Bruno himself had begun monastic life on the feast of the Baptist. Ludolf of Saxony called John the first hermit and founder of monastic life. Over the centuries, monastics have continued to look to John the Baptist for inspiration and patronage. John – prophet, ascetic, penitent, solitary – has been a prototype for those seeking God in monastic solitude and speaking to God in the silence of their hearts.

JESUS

Like all believing Christians, monastics of the Church have found in the person of Jesus of Nazareth an undying source of inspiration, a constant challenge and enigmatic model for living the gospel message conscientiously and efficaciously. Baptised into the life, death and resurrection of Christ, they have sought to mirror Christ, and, as much as possible, become Christ for others. That they should try to do so by consciously looking to the Jesus of solitude is not surprising. Jesus showed himself as the way and salvation. He told disciples to imitate his life, to live their own lives unto Golgotha selflessly, and to embrace the true freedom of his gospel teaching. He shared our human condition and cleared the way by no uncertain example.

Monastics have always known a close kinship with the Jesus who entered the desert wilderness to be tempted; who sought out mountaintops and solitary places for prayer; who stood transfigured on Mount Tabor; who prayed in solitude in Gethsemani garden; who died a lonely and painful death at another desolate place of execution. In all these places, Jesus was in communion with his Father. The real test for generations of monastics has been to embrace solitude as a locus for communion with and contemplation of God, rather than as a supposed escape from human suffering or the complications inherent in human relations. So the monastic heart has fixed its gaze on Jesus in his solitariness, to transform a contemplative moment in life into a contemplative movement of life, and to join its own contemplative gaze with that of Jesus in solitary contemplative union with the Father.

Mark's gospel account opens with a description of John the Baptist preaching his baptism of repentance, followed by Jesus' own baptism by John and his subsequent sojourn in the desert wilds where he underwent temptations. The Spirit 'drove' Jesus into the desert, according to the Marcan account. It would seem that Jesus probably did not need much coercing because he went there often during his public ministry to pray in solitude, get away from the crowds, and privately teach his band of disciples. Jesus moved into desert retreat to pray to God, to fathom God's will, and to experience temptations. His consent to God's will became especially clear when Jesus found himself on a mountaintop, tempted to throw himself into earthly power and prestige (Matt. 4:8–10). Jesus seemed to be as fond of mountaintops as of desert wilderness! He climbed the heights to pray in solitude. Luke tells us that Jesus habitually withdrew into isolated spots to pray, after tending to the needs of the crowds. We read that he prayed in solitude during the night (Mark 1:35), or even throughout the night (Luke 6:12). Malatesta suggests that Jesus only came to understand his unique vocation and his relationship to God within his experience of solitary prayer to the Father.[4]

In solitude Jesus could contemplate God's presence and will with concentrated effort. Jesus' solitary prayer nourished and strengthened him for his ministry to the crowds coming to be fed, nourished, healed, cured and made whole. He needed the solace of solitude in order to replenish his reserves and resolve. John Cassian wrote that Abba Isaac encouraged all to follow Jesus' example: 'Thus he taught us by the example of his withdrawal that, if we too wish to address God with purity and integrity of heart, we should likewise draw apart from all the turbulence and confusion of the crowd.'[5] But Jesus was not only solitary in prayer. Because he was so unique, he always stood apart in his unique calling. With whom could he possibly share his unique vision, awareness and experience? Although he could share some of his mystery with his apostles and closer disciples, Jesus' road to Jerusalem always lay ahead of him – paved with suffering, pain and abandonment.

On the way to Jerusalem, Jesus climbed another mountain, taking with him the apostles Peter, James and John. The astounding Taboric light manifested Jesus in all his glory as Son of God, speaking with those solitary prophets Moses and Elijah on either side of him. A heavenly voice claimed Jesus as God's Son, directing the apostles to listen to Jesus. Early monks and nuns adopted the transfiguration event as one of their primary focuses, hoping to be bathed in that transfiguring light with the Lord. And of course, 'listening to the Lord' has been a mainstay of monastic spirituality through *lectio divina* (sacred reading) throughout the centuries.

The events surrounding Jesus' betrayal, passion, death and resurrection in Jerusalem took place quickly, with a startling, relentless pace for the confused apostles and disciples. In Gethsemani Jesus prayed – once again in solitude – as the three privileged apostles from Mount Tabor slept nearby. He prayed in fear and loneliness. He was experiencing the fragility of human existence at its ultimate moment – death. Jesus was mostly silent during this process, until he experienced the silence of God at the moment of death. Then the earth was 'silent' in a harrowing way. The experience of the risen Christ in the Spirit necessarily includes Jesus' death; there is no resurrection without death. Entering the solitude of Jesus became a way for believers to commune with God vis-à-vis the universal aspirations and experiences of humanity. Entering Jesus' suffering and death allowed believers to unite themselves with the brokenness and loneliness of the human condition. Solitaries come to solidarity with the world especially in its brokenness, alienation and poverty.[6] Such was the example of Jesus of Nazareth; and such would become the pattern of life for dedicated believers, including Christian monastics.

MARY

Luke's gospel twice depicts the figure of Mary in a posture most amenable to monastic hearts of all ages. In Luke 2:19 Mary 'ponders in her heart' the events surrounding the birth of her child in Bethlehem. Once again, in Luke 2:51, Mary ponders in her 'heart' what happens when she discovers the adolescent Jesus in discussion with learned men in the Temple. Monastics are attracted to this silent, pondering woman who gives birth to Jesus, watches him grow and develop, gather disciples around himself in a startlingly public way, and suffer crucifixion by the Roman authorities at the request of his own people. At that moment her silence was complete, as she stood beneath her crucified son. But then, the Scriptures basically depict Mary as a silent woman. From the beginning of her greatest secret – the message of the angel Gabriel – she is silent. For whatever reason, she did not even tell Joseph about the epiphany she had experienced, but kept silence about the encounter. Among other attributes, Mary's reflective silence has been a model for monastic contemplatives from the earliest Christian roots of monasticism.

Regardless of any particular assumed critical interpretation of the Annunciation (e.g. a post-resurrection expression of the early Church's reflections about Jesus), the figure of Mary as contemplative and obedient to God's will remains an ideal with whose stance monastics can identify and try to mirror in their own lives. Mary responds to God's Word as later disciples were expected to respond to that Word. Although she hesitated somewhat at the meaning of such a momentous event for human history, Mary gave her assent. And at that unique moment, Mary cuts a very solitary figure, forging ahead on a journey into mystery. To discover that one is to become the mother of the long-awaited Messiah would surely place anyone in a pensive mood!

The Lucan infancy narratives next record Mary's trip to the hill country to visit her cousin Elizabeth, who was then experiencing her own momentous pregnancy. Mary was flush with her own remarkable experience. The baby in Elizabeth's womb leaped for joy. Mary proclaimed her Magnificat in the name of the *anawim* – the poor, rejected, marginals and outcasts of the people. From the beginning, the incarnation flips the tables of reality upside down. The monastic heart has long welcomed this gospel event, sanctifying already in Elizabeth's womb the life of John the Baptist, its desert forebear. And within the quiet, hidden life of Mary, monastics have celebrated with contemplative joy the mystery of God's Word coming into the world.

When Simeon met the infant Jesus in the Temple (Luke 2:25–35), he told Mary that a 'sword' would later pierce her heart (soul). Within the passion narrative of John's gospel account, Mary encountered that sword as she stood beneath Jesus' cross of crucifixion. Perhaps she had foreseen the inevitability of Jesus' death from her quiet perspective. Standing in the desolate pain of a mother watching her child's execution, Mary experienced her powerlessness. Before he died, Jesus entrusted Mary to the 'disciple he loved' as his mother, and the disciple to Mary as her son. Already in the early Church, theologians saw in this episode the entrustment of Mary to the believing community as mother. Mary, in contemplative stance beneath the cross, became the mother of the Church and indeed, mother of monks and nuns as well.

During the patristic era, the Church's theologians focused on Mary vis-à-vis the great salvific and ecclesial events contained in the gospels. But already then, the beginnings of a Marian spirituality were forming. Mary was not only 'Mother of God' but our mother as well, and as such, present in our lives in an ongoing way. For monks, Greek hymnists praised Mary's silence and solitude. For instance, the hymns of Mary's Presentation intended to invoke Mary as the model of Christian contemplation in her silent solitude. For the Greeks, Mary was the ideal monk.[7]

Later monks of the West developed a strong spirituality of Mary that centred on monastic communion with the Word of God vis-à-vis Mary's relationship to that Word. Marian spirituality, and indeed mysticism in monastic perspective, reached its height once again in the eleventh to thirteenth centuries. Both Benedictines and Cistercians helped this Marian mystique evolve, and it remained largely a monastic spirituality[8] until the mendicant orders fashioned a Marian piety more easily accessible to the laity. Some of the monastic commentaries on the Song of Songs used a Marian lens of interpretation (e.g. Rupert of Deutz[9] and John of Ford[10]). She became a monastic mirror for silence, solitude and contemplation.

4. SOLITUDE IN ATHANASIUS' *LIFE OF ANTONY*

St Athanasius was born *c*.296/7 in Alexandria, Egypt to Christian parents. He received an excellent education and, when he was 21, was ordained deacon and appointed secretary to Alexander, then Bishop of Alexandria. He helped lead the battle against Arius the Alexandrian and his Arian heresy, especially at the Council of Nicaea. Not long after this council, Alexander died and Athanasius became bishop. He quickly visited the monastic settlements within his diocese and formed bonds that would later serve him well. Athanasius found himself caught in the fourth-century seesaw between Arianism and orthodoxy, and was forced into exile five times. During his third and fourth exiles, Athansius lived with the monks of the Egyptian deserts and published much of his literary output, including his famous *Life of Antony*, a monk who had come to Athanasius' defence in his struggle against Arianism. During Athanasius' lifetime, monastic life spread remarkably.

Generally, scholars accept 357 as the date of composition for the *Life of Antony*, although some have suggested a much later date. Even the authorship has been disputed – as recently as the late nineteenth century[1] – but generally most critics today accept Athanasian authorship. Much of Athanasius' own ideas will be found in the text, placed in the words and teaching of his friend, the monk Antony. Athanasius was surely aware of Greek classical examples of biography, such as Porphyry's biography of Plotinus, his teacher. The forms of these biographies would likely have influenced him; just as more contemporary examples of 'sage' or 'hero' stories might well have figured in his approach to biography. But his Christian biography of Antony centres on its Christian content, thereby giving birth to a new genre in Christian literature.

In a sense, the *Life of Antony* became the 'how to' for writing Christian biography and hagiography. Its fame spread quickly and, hailed by many important Christian voices, it became the classic it remains today in Christian and monastic spirituality. Biographers of monks clearly began to use the *Life* as their model for framing the words and deeds of monastic saints. Although Antony was reportedly an unlettered fellow, we do have a small corpus of letters dictated by him to other monks and monastic settlements, as well as mention of still other letters sent to monastic communities. We also have collected sayings of Antony contained in the *Apophthegmata*, collected sayings of the fourth-century desert monastics. There are certain nuances about Antony that come through these sayings. Bringing these sources together – *Life of Antony*, letters and apophthegms – we have more than inklings about an amazing, saintly monk.

Anachoresis was the term used in fourth-century Egypt for tax evasion by means of flight. People who could not afford to pay oppressive taxes, as well as officials who could not pay those duties for which they were personally responsible during their time in office, would simply move elsewhere. Many Egyptian farmers turned to *anachoresis* as their only solution, either by becoming the disaffected 'drop-outs' of society, or finding a situation wherein someone else would be financially responsible. Authorities were afraid that these fugitives might band together into motivated mobs. The phenomenon of desert monasticism in fourth-century Egypt found root in this context of *anachoresis*.

'Monks', 'apotactics' and 'anchorites' were all terms used to refer to the Christian ascetics who were moving into the deserts. For the most part, the monastic 'anchorites', however, were not hiding from authorities. In the movement's beginning, they lived just outside towns and villages, and only moved into the desert wastelands and mountain wilderness at a later point. 'Apoctactic' seems to have referred to urban ascetics who rejected marriage and banded together, but still lived in a way connected to society. *Monachos* or 'monk' became a term referring to all types of Christian desert ascetics. Before long, monastics formed their own societies that interacted with, and found recognition by, the wider civil society. Once they had moved into the desert wastes, monks built cells and places to gather for prayer, monastic buildings and settlements. Samuelson refers to monasticism's emergence as desert urbanisation – a point Athanasius makes in the *Life of Antony* (#14).[2]

Who was the monk Antony? Tradition holds that he was born in 251 at the village of Coma, in the Nile valley of Middle Egypt. His was a Coptic Christian household in which he, his younger sister and their parents lived a life of relative ease; they were landowners. Antony's parents both died when he was between eighteen and twenty, leaving him the care of a much younger sister. He seems to have been a shy, retiring youth, preferring to spend time with his parents in the local church than to pursue an education or even friendships with other youths. While pondering in church one day the description of the early Christian community banded around the apostle in Acts 4, he heard the gospel text about selling all possessions in order to be perfect (Matt. 19:21). Antony then gave away his land and sold his possessions, giving the land to his fellow villagers and the money to the poor, except for that set aside for his sister.

But once more he heard the gospel text in church about not worrying about tomorrow (Matt. 6:34), so he gave away the rest of his possessions and entrusted his little sister to the care of a group of dedicated virgins. He sought out an ascetic near his village and learned what he could from this 'spiritual master', while devoting himself to ascetical practices and continual prayer. He then spent a period of years in solitude among the nearby tombs in the desert until he was about thirty-five (*c*.285). After unsuccessfully trying to convince his former spiritual master to join him in the desert, Antony moved into an abandoned fort across the Nile for some twenty years, where he lived in solitude on bread (supplied twice a year by friends) and water. Others who wanted to live an ascetical life with Antony came and broke into his fortress of solitude (*c*.305). He emerged from his solitude as a healer, teacher and spiritual master, who encouraged many others to take up solitary desert life.

Now called Deir-el-Meimoun,[3] this mountain of Pispir (Antony's 'exterior' mountain) served him as a place for solitude as well as active ministry to the monastic ascetics gathering around him. Later he would temporarily leave this sanctuary to minister to Christian slaves in the mines and prisons, who were awaiting martyrdom during the persecution of Maximin. He also visited neighbouring monastic settlements, at their request. Then he retreated to a place of greater solitude (his 'interior' mountain) in the mountainous region of Quolzoûn, in a wadi about nineteen miles from the Red Sea – now the monastery of Deir-amba-Antonios. Disciples would visit him there and he, in turn, would occasionally return to Pispir to visit his disciples, to teach and to minister. But this final solitude was essentially a time of deepening holiness and discernment. He died there in 356 and was buried by two disciples sworn to secrecy regarding his tomb's location.

Like all the great monastic founders and reformers, Antony embraced asceticism as the way to condition the body and discipline the mind so as to open the heart to contemplative prayer. Fasting, vigils, continuous prayer, reading Scripture, a regimen of manual labour conducive to prayer, and a generally austere lifestyle characterised his ascetical approach. Silence and solitude pervaded his asceticism. Antony's goal was union with God, the search for which drew him progressively deeper into experiences of solitude. By his later years, Antony's asceticism and contemplative prayer had formed him into a spiritual master sought out by many from all walks of life. Antony gives a nice summation of learned asceticism in what has been designated his letter #1. There he lists the classic monastic virtues and practices: perseverance, obedience, repentance, asceticism, prayer, fasting, renunciation, humility and contrition.[4]

Antony's life illustrates the contemplative heart's passage from solitude to deeper solitude. Étienne Bettencourt[5] has schematised the four 'flights' of Antony into greater solitude – the four phases of his hermit existence. The first phase (*Life* chs 2–7) describes Antony living ascetically first at home, under the instruction of an older ascetic just outside the village. There he devotes himself to prayer and fasting, as well as to fighting the demons of temptation. The second phase (*Life* chs 8–10) takes Antony away from the village to the desert tombs, where he lives in solitude and applies himself to an intensified battle with the demons. One of the apophthegms ascribed to Antony may further elucidate the nature of this battle, when he says that the desert-dweller escapes three problems (hearing, speech and sight), but there is still fornication.[6]

The third phase (*Life* chs 11–48) places Antony at the abandoned desert fort where he suffers through greater temptations in solitude and emerges a spiritual master who attracts and teaches many disciples, while hoping for his total personal commitment in martyrdom. He urges his disciples to maintain faithfully the discipline of solitude. Again, from the apophthegms, Antony is reputed to have said that monks outside the cell are like fish out of water. They should run back to their cells like fish swimming towards the sea. Otherwise, they will lose their vigilance.[7] The fourth and final phase (*Life* chs 49–88) describes Antony's life in the 'interior' mountain, where fruits of solitude champion him as an athlete of Christ who endures all hardship and a 'man of God' who fights heresy, heals others, performs miracles and is a model of wisdom and grace. So Antony's journey can be envisaged as a passage from one solitude to ever more remote solitudes.

Though called forth from his solitude from time to time – to visit his monks at Pispir, to care for prisoners, to fight heresy and to minister to others – Antony was faithful to his solitary call. He was praying in his 'inner' mountain.[8] He was maintaining a vigilant heart.[9] He needed the solitude that fashioned him into a spiritual master, but he also needed periodically to come out of solitude into ministry, out of love. Bouyer adds that authentic Christian solitude will always bear fruits of love.[10]

In an age when martyrdom became less likely, due to a gradual Christianisation of the Empire, the desert became a locus for a type of martyrdom. Desert monastics suffered a 'white' martyrdom, Christian apologists would say – white in opposition to the bloody red of physical martyrdom. Later on, the expression 'green' martyrdom would be coined in reference to exilic peregrinations assumed by Celtic monks. During the fourth century, men and women moved into desert wastelands to take on this 'white' martyrdom. Antony unsuccessfully pursued martyrdom during Maximin's persecution, so he became instead a 'martyr of love' in the Egyptian desert.

Like Antony, his disciples in the desert adopted a life of general solitude, with opportunities to visit and pray with other solitaries around them. Even Antony, though he had experienced protracted periods of total solitude during his earlier years, never lived in total isolation. Those who embraced Antony's anchoritic ideal did so, usually, within a colony of solitaries. Antony and contemporaries viewed the desert wilderness as the stronghold of demonic forces. The desert was a place of desolation and death, the perfect place for the 'Lord of this world' and all demonic spirits to rule. Christian ascetics moved away from inhabited areas into the wilderness so they could do solitary battle against such demons. Antony intentionally challenged demons by entering 'their' space. Those who followed him into the desert con-sciously joined this warfare. The battle was to pray constantly; fight distractions and temptations; confront evil; supplant all the complex inroads of evil with clear and simple paths of virtuous living; purify the heart and remain at peace.

The *Life of Antony* is filled with allusions to demons and descriptions of Antony's own struggles with demonic forces in his life. This can prove rather unpalatable for many modern readers because they are used to thinking in psychological terms about the struggle undergone by Antony in solitude, not

in terms of demons. Everyone must come to terms with evil in
life, whether one describes this struggle in psychological jargon
or by demonic depiction. Solitude is a gateway to the inner life
and, no matter what language one uses to discuss the conflicts and struggles of that world within, the experience of
entering the fray is deeply human and shared by those who
make the passage. Antony blazed a trail for that journey in a
very vivid way. His solitude was not, for the most part, a quiet,
taciturn solitude, but noisy with taunting demons and dra-
matic struggles.

Athanasius tells us that 'everyone' referred to Antony as the
'man of God', a title traditionally given to prophets such as
Moses, Elijah and John the Baptist. In fact, Athanasius points
out parallels between Antony and those other desert prophets.
In his letter #6, Antony himself encourages his disciples to
complete devotion to God by harkening to Elijah's sacrifice on
Mount Carmel. Antony is a 'man of God' also because he imi-
tates Jesus by his temptations in the wilderness. As with
Jesus, the Spirit drives Antony into the desert wilderness to
be tempted; like Jesus, Antony overcomes temptation and is
filled with the Holy Spirit. Antony – Christlike 'man of God'
and prophet – became an icon of solitude for his disciples and
for monastics down the centuries.

Though Antony's life was marked by simplicity, austerity
and especially solitude, he was not a confirmed recluse. Once
he had monastic disciples in the desert at Pispir and the desert
became a 'city', Antony actively ministered to them as spiritual
abba. Even when he had moved to his 'interior' mountain for
greater solitude, monks came to him regularly for teaching
and advice. He left his solitude to minister to prisoners, to
battle against Arianism in Alexandria, to perform cures and
visit neighbouring monastic settlements. Far from being a tire-
some burden that disturbed monastic solitude, Antony's
ministries complemented his life of prayer and contemplation.
The potential for dilemma in the dialectic of action/contem-
plation does not seem to ignite in Antony. He is a spiritual

father to the end and goes about the noble business of cultivating the hearts of monastic saints with an admirable zeal.

Athanasius seems to suggest that Antony's solitude was not
antithetical to his ministry, but even a positive force strength-
ening him for that ministry. He repeatedly comes forth from
solitude empowered to teach, direct, heal and troubleshoot
for those seeking his guidance. After active ministry, Antony
returns to the solace of his monastic solitude. This balance of
action and contemplation vis-à-vis the solitary life will be a
constant thread running through the fabric of monastic solitude throughout history. It is not simply a 'problem' for
solitaries to tackle, or 'issue' to debate. The action/contem-
plation balance would help to determine the various
articulations of how monastic solitude could be envisioned and
lived. Indeed, it is difficult to think of the question anywhere
but at the very core of monastic (or any other) spirituality.

Antony had many disciples and followers during his monastic life. Athanasius tells us that Antony encouraged many
others to become solitaries.[11] Ammonas, Amoun, Hilarion and
Macarius are perhaps more famous than others. We have the
letters of Ammonas, Antony's successor. Reading his words
of direction about solitude, we can easily see the influence of
Antony's life and teaching. He writes that we cannot see God
until we separate ourselves from all distractions, when we
recognise our adversary.[12] That is why Elijah and John the
Baptist withdrew into their desert solitudes, he writes, so they
could be quiet and receive God's power.[13] Those who cannot
keep quiet will not be able to overcome their passions or fight
the adversary, because their passions will get in the way.[14]

But Antony's influence went far beyond the Egyptian
deserts. Athanasius' biography of Antony moved 'hero' literature into the realm of Christian spirituality. His aim was to
set an ideal within a general biographical framework. Antony's
life became not only a benchmark for other Christian monastics, but also a critical reference point for other
hagiographers. His fame spread through Athanasius, Evagrius
and John Cassian in the West. Leclercq[15] points out that Peter

Damian and the Romualdians especially harkened to Antony's life. Rudolf of Camaldoli also invoked, in 1080, the memory of those solitary desert saints: 'the Pauls and the Antonys, successors of the prophets'.[16]

The spiritual themes and teachings contained in the *Life of Antony* became the ideal for all monastics, regardless of particular tradition. Antony speaks to monastic life itself. That is why monastic founders and reformers during the centuries – from Benedictines to Camaldolese to Carthusians and Cistercians – would look to Antony the Great as the great patriarch of the desert and the true 'father' of monastic solitude.

5. DESERT SOLITUDE: *LIVES* AND *SAYINGS* OF DESERT SOLITARIES

The monastic phenomenon sprang up not only in the Egyptian desert regions with Antony the Great and his followers, but similar movements also took root in Syria and Cappadocia (present-day Turkey) on the margins of society almost simultaneously with Egypt's experience. Soon Palestinian monasticism would also take shape, as well as the early monastic foundations in the West – those of Honoratus of Lérins, Caesarius of Arles and John Cassian, near Marseilles. Although many moved into the desert for mixed motives, especially where taxation and military conscription were concerned, others journeyed there for expressly religious purposes, such as living a 'white' martyrdom, responding radically to gospel mission, and becoming an ascetical 'athlete' for Christ. The written records left by the desert *abbas* and *ammas* form a remarkable body of literature testifying to their spiritual asceticism and evident holiness.

Why the desert? Why the margins of society, the frontiers? Abba Antony and his monastic brothers and sisters of subsequent generations moved into the open spaces of wilderness to know a solitude only a few had previously enjoyed. Rufinus described the desert wilderness of Scetis as a vast desert and great silence, with monks in solitary cells.[1] Romanticised notions of this desert existence abound, as do the inflated numbers of supposed desert-dwellers, but we do know that a significant number of ascetics eked out a difficult life there, alone or in small groups, and later, in large organised communities. One of the old abbas was Abba Elias, who lived in the desert of Antinoë in the Thebaid, renowned for having lived decades in the remotest desert which even the other desert ascetics considered 'rugged' and which he never left to visit the more inhabited areas.[2]

As Antony had waged desert warfare with the demons in his various solitudes, subsequent desert monastics also became ascetical warriors. Abba John the Dwarf advised others to stay in their cells and become aware of their thoughts, as he did, and to find refuge by praying to God for help.[3] Many of these solitaries felt themselves plagued by demonic forces with which they had to contend on a daily basis. Abba John of Lycopolis related how he felt besieged by demons day and night, unable to pray or sleep throughout the night as a progression of images tortured him.[4] Abba Evagrius of Pontus agreed that the mind is difficult to keep in control when one is so burdened with fantasies.[5]

But these desert ascetics had to contend with more than 'demons' in the desert. Extremes of temperature, aridity, blowing sand, lack of fresh water, murderous Berbers, wild animals: all joined forces to make monastic desert life difficult, at best. Abba Didymus[6] was renowned for killing various poisonous reptiles by stamping on them with his bare feet. Evidently others tried to imitate him, dying from the venom.[7] Abba Theon took a different approach to relating with the animals, befriending his quadruped neighbours and giving them feed and water during the night hours, so that other ascetics noticed all their tracks around Theon's cell in the morning. Theon took utter delight in the animals, creating his own peaceable kingdom.[8] Nevertheless, desert solitude was (and is) not something to take lightly. It was a hard, challenging lifestyle for anyone. The desert is a perilous place fraught with dangers that do not even enter our 'civilised' consciousness.

Around 400, the desert was in upheaval in Egypt, due to the Origenist controversy pitting monk against monk and leading to the expulsions of many monks after Origen's condemnation in Alexandria. Another catastrophe struck in 407–8 when the region of Scetis was devastated by hordes of marauding nomads. Many abbas were slaughtered, such as Abba Moses and those gathered around him. Another wave of desert solitaries left the Egyptian deserts for those of Palestine. Most of those remaining in Egypt formed cenobitic groups or joined extant monasteries.

After the devastating events at the turn of the century and early fifth century, there was a movement to memorialise the words and deeds of the fourth-century monastics. The various collections of the sayings (*Apophthegmata*) began to form. Rufinus finished his rendition of an existing travelogue/report (*The History of the Monks of Egypt*) a few years after the destruction in Scetis. Around 420, Palladius wrote his *Lausiac History* and John Cassian his *Conferences of the Fathers* and *Institutes of the Cenobia*. After the golden age of Scetis (and even before), desert monastics saw themselves as descendants of the great masters. The oral transmission and later written records of desert wisdom became crucial to the historical development and spiritual sustenance of monasticism.

The various collections of desert sayings tried to encapsulate wisdom personified in those revered men and women of the desert. The *Apophthegmata* were, from the beginning, more than merely quaint stories or clever words. The meaning behind the stories or within the words was designed for practical use, for imitation. The men and women whose 'sayings' were collected continued on in tradition as the great heroes and heroines showing the path for others. This was also true for the *Lives* written by Palladius, Rufinus and others. Withdrawal or 'flight' from the world was a key element in the desert tradition. To leave family, friends and, indeed, civilisation behind and enter desert solitude was really the first step and first test for the aspirant. Fleeing (people, speech and the world) became a consistent refrain of advice in the desert. This sounds antisocial and misanthropic to us, but Abba Theodore of Pherme qualifies the advice by adding that one flees neighbour to the cell for refuge, but never out of hatred.[9] In later monastic literature, one encounters the phrase 'contempt (or hatred) for the world', but rarely in the desert literature. Even when the concept 'hatred' appears, it usually means renunciation. And yet, withdrawal from society was very much a part of the monastic impulse.

They withdrew from society and moved into the wilderness, seeking solitude. They wanted to be 'alone with the Alone'.[10] People moved into the desert to be alone, together. Many of the early desert pioneers came to resemble biblical prophets to their disciples and later generations. Monastic tradition held them to be the direct descendants of the great desert heroes, Elijah and John the Baptist. Many women also moved into the desert for solitude and silence. Although the collections of 'sayings' include only three ammas among all those abbas, surely it is significant that they were included at all! Some were former prostitutes, while others had been *parthenoi* – dedicated virgins in society. Still other women were pilgrims who came to the desert and simply stayed. At times, women came for healing or spiritual direction, or for any of the reasons their male counterparts had used to make the move. That the men who considered these women to be embodied temptation would have welcomed their presence in the desert is unlikely. Those early ammas became adept at hiding their sex. There are many stories in the literature about how, at his death, an abba was discovered to be an amma.

Three ammas are included in the alphabetical series of *Sayings*: Syncletica, Theodora and Sara. Syncletica was one who, interestingly, did not hide her sex. She simply lived in desert simplicity and, early on, her wisdom was recognised. Theodora lived in the desert of Scetis, and even the abbas came to this powerful desert amma for advice.[11] Amma Sarah lived on a river bank in the desert of Pelusium. She ministered to a monastery of women nearby and, unlike Syncletica and Theodora, felt forced to justify her desert life to the abbas. Amma Matrona was a desert amma about whom we know little. Two of her 'sayings' also appear in some of the versions of *Apophthegmata*, one of which admits that many desert ascetics have missed the point by trying to live as if they were still in the world: better to live with others and desire solitude than to have it while wanting to be elsewhere![12] Just as the men joined forces and formed communities for many reasons, so the desert women also formed monastic communities. In fact, early on, the women tended to band together for mutual support and protection. But solitude and silence remained elements in all desert spirituality.

Solitude in the desert tradition is a refuge and a great respite. It makes possible the right kind of atmosphere for union and communion. The simpler the surroundings, the less cluttered will be the mind and heart. The desert forces the mind to clear and the heart to open. Abba Arsenius could think of no better way: solitude, silence and peace.[13] The locus for monastic solitude became the cell, whether a cave, tomb, hut, hole, or room in a building. There the classic spiritual combat occurred, where monastics placed their human weakness in God's power and life. There they faced their inner demons in the battle for truth. In the cell the monk or nun would plant the roots of stability and perseverance, come what may. For the early anchorites and semi-anchorites, the cell was where life was lived – prayer, work, meals, sleep. Hospitality was also a chief concern in the desert, so they visited one another. Many of the most famous 'sayings' are derived from such visits. Disciples regularly visited their abbas for spiritual direction. Monks also had to attend to occasional pilgrims and visitors, tourists and would-be monks. But generally, they spent most of their time in the cell. Typical advice would be simply to sit in the cell, live there as simply as possible, and be mindful of one's sinfulness, praying for salvation. Besides, the cell will teach one everything one needs to know.[14]

But staying in the cell was only the beginning of the combat. Sitting in the cell for days, weeks, months, years and a lifetime was difficult. But it was the place for the monastics to encounter God in solitude. It was *the* way for a desert solitary to be. Towards the end of the fourth century, it was no longer enough simply to stay in the cell. How one lived in the cell became more crucial. One could devote a lifetime to the cell without really learning how to live in the cell.[15] The desert cell was no romanticised utopia, but a simple place of encounter and discovery.

It may seem ironic to be paying so much attention to the words of those desert ascetics who tried so diligently to be, above all, silent. But they conversed with God in that silence and the fruits of those long conversations were their famous sayings and deeds. Many of the abbas taught their disciples desert wisdom by their example of silence. The key immediate lesson to learn was that, until they attained an inner stillness through their exercise of silence, they would not really be able to focus on their weakness and entrust it to God's care. Abba Pambo felt that people should be edified by a monk's silence rather than by his impressive words.[16] This and similar desert wisdom about silence shows how silence protected monks from gossip, prejudice, turmoil and uncharitableness. Positively put, the language of silence also helped them to focus, to be present, to be mindful of God's enduring presence. But the proof is in the pudding. How did this mindfulness and contemplative union translate into life's relationships, community and church life? Abba Serinus said that if one lives outside the cell as he lives inside it, then he is on the right path.[17]

Some of the abbas moved out of anchoritic solitude into a semi-eremitic or even cenobitic lifestyle. After the great decimation of desert monks in 407, more monks moved to relatively safer environs behind monastery walls. There did not seem to be the extreme antipathy between the anchorites and the cenobites that erupted from time to time in later monastic history. Which lifestyle was appropriate became a matter of discernment for each desert ascetic. Abba Joseph of Panephysis advised that, if one is at home both in a cenobitic setting and a hermit's cell, then one should discern where one would make the most profit and thrive, and live there.[18] Deep inner peace, communion with God, and unceasing prayer lay at the core of desert monastic solitude and silence, however these disciplines might be personally articulated.

PART TWO: THEOLOGY AND DIALECTIC

6. SOLITUDE IN SELECTED MONASTIC PATRISTIC SOURCES

This chapter will examine cursorily the place solitude held in the lives and works of ten representative patristic writers. All ten were monks, though some later became bishops. Here are proponents of monastic solitude from Cappadocia, Egypt, Gaul, Syria, Palestine and Sinai. During these early years of monasticism, theologies of monastic life were forming. Certain issues, like solitude, sometimes became the source of controversy and polemic, especially when the issue of excess was involved.

BASIL THE GREAT

Basil the Great sprang from prodigiously saintly stock. His paternal grandmother, who raised and largely tutored him, was Macrina the Elder. She and her husband had reportedly hid in the forest for many years while enduring religious persecution. His parents were St Basil the Elder and St Emmelia, whose father had been martyred during an imperial persecution. When Basil's father died, Emmelia joined her daughter, St Macrina the Younger, as solitaries of Pontus. A community of virgins later formed around them in the Isis River valley. Basil's brothers were Sts Gregory of Nyssa and Peter of Sebaste – both bishops – and Naucratius who died accidentally while living as a solitary in the Pontic wilderness. Peter led a male community also on the family property of Annisa near the Isis River, before succeeding the famous Eustathius of Sebaste as bishop.

Basil was educated in Caesarea before pursuing further

classical studies in Athens with fellow students Gregory Nazianzus and the future emperor, Julian the Apostate. He then
travelled to see first-hand the desert ascetics in Egypt, Mesopotamia, Palestine and Syria – a journey evidently suggested by
Eustathius, an ascetic who had befriended the family and was
particularly close to Macrina, Emmelia and the community
formed around them. Holmes refers to the controversial Eustathius as the *éminence grise*[1] of monastic life in Cappadocia.
Basil would later have to distance himself from Eustathius
whose moral and monastic teachings would effectively separate from orthodox tradition. But after visiting the desert
monks, Basil likely found their Cappadocian counterpart in
Eustathius. Basil later wrote to monks (probably in Pontus),
warning them against those who were confusing them in their
solitary life, and encouraged them to keep their faith and not
rely solely on asceticism.[2]

When Basil returned from his monastic 'pilgrimage', he went
to Annisa where he embraced a monastic life across the Isis
River from his sister Macrina, quite possibly at Naucratius'
former retreat. At different times he was joined there by his
brother Gregory and Gregory Nazianzus, the latter never truly
taking to the life at Anissa, though he would later 'wax
romantic' about his experience there. While together at Anissa,
Basil and Gregory Nazianzus composed the *Philokalia* – an
anthology of Origen – and the *Moral Rules*, an early attempt
to regulate life at Anissa. There Basil composed his 'short'
Asceticon – a series of questions and answers about monastic
asceticism. When he founded a monastery in Caesarea after
he became bishop, Basil wrote an expanded version for his
monastic disciples back at Pontus. He had succeeded his
patron Eusebius to the see of Caesarea in 370.

In Rule #6 of his *Long Rules* Basil wrote that secluded
locations help to remove distractions.[3] He had an appreciation
for monastic solitude. Much earlier, he had written to Gregory
Nazianzus from Annisa, stating that the only way to escape
distractions was to completely separate oneself from the world
and seek solitude's quieting effect on the soul.[4] He wrote once

again to Gregory from Anissa, extolling its wonderful location for growing all kinds of fruit, but especially the sweetest fruit of them all – solitude.[5] Solitude for prayer and silent reflection was one thing, but eremitical solitude was something entirely different for Basil.

The Basil who wrote the *Long Rules* was very different from the Basil who lived as a hermit at Anissa. Rule #7 is famous for its denunciation of hermits, warning how the hermit is only concerned with his own needs and cannot live the law of love. The hermit cannot see his own faults and has no way of showing humility, compassion, or service.[6] Why did Basil turn so vociferously against hermits? Perhaps he looked back on his Annisa period with dismay. In the same letter (#2) to Gregory in which he stressed the need for solitude, Basil wrote that he was personally having a difficult time dealing with solitude. He seemed not to know what to do with himself. He had not escaped his passions and distractions, and he admitted that he was not benefiting from solitude.[7] Was he 'wasting' his time at Anissa? Was he reacting against the eremitism in his own family? Was he attempting to counteract the influence of Eustathius on Cappadocian monasticism? Was he rejecting the extremes he witnessed among Syrian ascetics? Whatever his motivation, it is clear that Basil considered hermit life a self-satisfied, self-preoccupied extreme. Basilian solitude will be found within the context of community.

Basil's monasticism was marked by its moderation. Perhaps that is why the Basilian rules and monastic customs were so successful, both in the East and the West. Eremitism generally continued to enjoy popularity in the East, especially in the 'laura' form of solitude in Palestinian and later Athonite monasticism. But in the West, other than Camaldolese and Carthusian 'laura' approaches to monastic solitude, eremitical solitude found staunch opposition – due in great part to Basil's influence. For Basil, communal life followed the example of the apostolic community found in Acts 2:44 and 4:32. He steered towards the middle ground between the anchorite's cave and the city's bustle. He urged the commandment of love upon his followers in monastic regulations. With Basilian monasticism, one can begin to speak of urban monasticism and 'restrained solitude' in the city.

EVAGRIUS OF PONTUS

Evagrius was born *c*.345 at Ibora in Pontus, not far from Basil's family estate. His father was a minor bishop of that locality, directly under the Bishop of Nyssa. He may well have known Basil's family early on. We do know that he became a disciple of Bishop Basil of Caesarea, who ordained him lector and served as Evagrius' mentor until his death in 379, at which time Gregory Nazianzus ordained him deacon. Evagrius would thereafter consider Gregory his master. Gregory took Evagrius with him to Constantinople when he became its bishop, making Evagrius archdeacon. When he resigned, Gregory entrusted Evagrius to Nectarios, his successor. Evagrius grew to social prominence and became accustomed to a rich urban life. When he became infatuated with a married woman, Evagrius precipitously fled the city on a ship bound for Palestine.

In Jerusalem, Melania and Rufinus at the monastery on the Mount of Olives welcomed him. Evagrius had undoubtedly studied Origen in Cappadocia. Both Melania and Rufinus were disciples of Origen. When Evagrius soon became seriously ill, Melania intuited his inner turmoil and advised him to live the monastic life in the Egyptian desert with some Origenist solitaries she knew there. Evagrius regained his health and took her advice. At Nitria, he lived in the most famous monastic centre in that desert. Later, at 'The Cells' he was able to live the greater solitude he sought, some eighteen kilometres south of Nitria. There he could live a semi-eremitical life in a cell not far from others – praying and working alone during the week, while joining the weekend communal worship and agape meal.

Evagrius was in contact with both Macarii, the Alexandrian serving as priest in 'The Cells' and the 'Great' who founded a colony of hermits at Scetis. He also knew Didymus the Blind, another devotee of Origen and renowned scriptural exegete who had taught in Alexandria such famous pupils as Jerome and Rufinus. For manual labour, Evagrius copied manuscripts and wrote his own works. What a literary output he accomplished in his personal synthesis of Greek wisdom and Coptic desert wisdom! For our purposes, we are concerned with the more distinctly monastic works: the *Praktikos*, the *Antirrhetikos, Ad Monachos, Chapters on Prayer*, his *Letters*, and *Treatise on the Eight Deadly Thoughts*. Some of these works will be found under the name St Nilus, allowing the Evagrian tradition to continue in the East after the Second Council of Constantinople condemned Evagrius as an Origenist. Evagrius' more doctrinal works that clearly expose him as Origenist are not really pertinent here.

To a great extent, Evagrius' desert wisdom echoes that of the other desert ascetics around him. But Evagrius' own intellectual background and obvious capabilities make his echoes resound with a fuller resonance and clarity. He added his own grasp of the human psyche and desert wisdom to the teachings of Origen, Basil and Gregory Nazianzus, giving the monks around him many practical ways to live their monastic desert life. With Evagrius, we resume our battle with the demons that openly fight the solitaries through thought processes. Monks must attain a state of peace – *hesychia* – in the solitude and silence of desert life, but they must always be vigilant for demons trying to prevent or destroy such peace.

Separation from the world and solitude in silence were key realities for Evagrius, but conditioned by love. It is better, he wrote, to be in a vast crowd in love, than to be alone in one's cave with bitterness and hatred.[8] Like Basil, Evagrius placed the onus of the law of love upon the shoulders of the hermit, but he was writing for hermits who had others around them. Known for his personal asceticism, Evagrius urged others to live likewise: fasting, work and solitude will extinguish desire.[9] But he was quick to caution moderation and timeliness.[10] The important practice was faithful solitude in the cell.

The 'noonday demon' or spirit of *acedia* was, for Evagrius, one of the eight deadly 'thoughts' he described for his fellow solitaries, and from which the medieval 'seven deadly sins' derived. *Acedia* turned the monk towards dejection, depression and, ultimately, despair. Solitude, tears and prayers are the recourse. Evagrius also urged the women of the desert to battle this demon with tears and prayers in the night.[11] It was important to maintain solitude and prayer life, in love. Evagrius, former disciple of Basil, answered the latter's charge against hermits by stating that a real monk, though separate from all, is united to all.[12] Evagrius likened the hermit separating himself from the world in order to meet God, to the desert experience of Christ. In that experience, the hermit encounters the world in the presence of Christ.[13]

The desert message of Abba Evagrius moved beyond 'The Cells' of Egypt, perhaps by way of Palladius or some travellers to Palestine and Syria. But Evagrian literary works did indeed spread throughout the monastic world. John Cassian never mentioned Evagrius, though he used his monastic doctrine, particularly on the 'eight deadly thoughts' and prayer. Maximus the Confessor also used Evagrian material in his works for the East. Syrians translated Evagrius, both under his own name and under the pseudonym Nilus. Despite those condemnations of some of his Origenist teachings, Evagrius of Pontus gave us, as Bouyer points out, the first whole system of Christian spirituality.[14] This spiritual heritage affected not only monastic circles but also the very development of Christian ascetical theology. Evagrian solitude proved most fruitful for articulating the spiritual journey and inner life of prayer.

EUCHERIUS OF LYONS

Born *c*.380, Eucherius married Galla and they had two sons, Salonius and Veranus. When his children were ten and eight respectively, Eucherius and Galla decided to abandon their property and livelihood and embrace lives of solitude. Since Eucherius was noble and perhaps even a senator in Gaul, this was no trifle. Though he evidently wished to visit the Egyptian desert monks, Eucherius decided against the trip, deferring to his young sons. All four moved to the isle of Lérins where the couple entrusted their sons to the care of the monks Hilary, Salvian and Vincent.[15] After some time at the monastery of Honoratus on Lérins, Eucherius entered a solitary life – as did Galla – on the nearby island of Léro (now Sainte-Marguerite) in the grotto of Cap-Roux. There he wrote *In Praise of the Desert* and *On Contempt for the World and Secular Philosophy.* His fame spread quickly enough for the people and clergy of Lyons to choose him as their nineteenth bishop *c*.435. During his episcopacy, he wrote two exegetical commentaries dedicated to his sons who would both become bishops. He had maintained correspondence with Honoratus, Paulinus of Nola and John Cassian.[16] Eucherius died *c*.450.

On Contempt is an exhortation to embrace gospel principles. *In Praise of the Desert* is a rhapsodic celebration of solitude and contemplative life – dedicated to Hilary of Lérins as he returned to the island's monastic solitude after a period away at Arles with Bishop Honoratus. Eucherius tells how admirable is his love of solitude to be returning to Lérins, showing that his love of God in solitude comes before all else.[17] The work is a jewel of monastic spirituality in which Eucherius recalls biblical desert connections: Moses on Sinai; the forty years in the desert; David fleeing Saul; Elijah in the desert; Elisha picking up the mantle; John the Baptist in the desert; Jesus in the desert; the transfigured Christ. He mentions Abba John, Abba Macarius and the other desert abbas.

Eucherius' spirituality is a continuation of the desert spirituality perpetuated in the *Lives* and *Sayings* of the desert monastics. Familiar themes reappear: separation from the world; battle against the vices; becoming virtuous; solitude; silence; incessant prayer; fasting and other asceticisms; reading and study of Scripture. But this desert life does not simply engender a masculine 'warrior' mentality; the feminine side of the desert carries solitaries as in a womb while they yearn for birth into eternal life.[18] He rhapsodises about how wonderful it is for those who thirst for God to be in solitude where even the silence of the natural world encourages the watching and waiting soul.[19]

Eucherius evokes the spousal spirituality of contemplative union by quoting from the Song of Songs 3:4, holding on to the beloved and never letting go.[20] He closes his 'song' of the desert by praising the 'desert' of Lérins itself and its spiritual progeny by name. Eucherius of Lyons encapsulated the desert spirituality of Egypt in his beautiful treatise on solitude. Some of the early monks of Lérins were exiles from those very deserts whose cells had been destroyed at the beginning of the century. As we shall see in John Cassian, desert wisdom found new ground in the West.

JOHN CASSIAN

John Cassian dedicated the second section of his *Conferences* (*Conf.* IX–XVII) to Eucherius. Cassian was born *c*.360 probably in one of the outlying Roman provinces near the Balkans. Though there is good reason to assume Cassian might have been native to Provence, there seems to be no pressing reason why we should not accept the testimony of Gennadius, a fifth-century citizen of present-day Marseilles, about '*Cassianus natione Scytha*'. This province of Sythia Minor (present-day Romania) would have accorded Cassian the bilingual education in Latin and Greek that has perplexed some scholars.

He and his close friend Germanus entered the monastic life *c*.380 in a cenobium near Bethlehem where they met Abba Pinufius from Egypt who was on one of his escapes from being the superior of a monastic group. Reluctantly, their Bethlehem superiors gave Cassian and Germanus permission to set out for Egypt to meet with cenobitic and eremitical abbas. After a prolonged stay there that had evidently not been the original plan, they returned to Bethlehem to make peace with their superiors and obtain permission to return to Egyptian monastic life. After another period in Egypt during which they finished their visits to Scetis and Nitria, the two monks made their way to John Chrysostom in Constantinople, just ahead of the culmination of the Origenist crisis.

Chrysostom welcomed them, ordaining Germanus, the older of the two, priest, and Cassian deacon. Under an anti-Origenist banner, Chrysostom himself was deposed and exiled; his cathedral, over whose treasury Cassian and Germanus had kept watch, was burned to the ground. The two monks travelled to Rome to plead Chrysostom's cause before Pope Innocent I. While in Rome, Cassian became a close friend of the future Pope Leo the Great. At some point, Cassian moved to Provence and Bishop Castor of Apt asked him (now an ordained priest) to found a monastic community. Although monastic foundations already existed, Castor recognised the need for monastic regulations and a balanced approach to Gallic monasticism. Cassian's desert years evidently fulfilled Castor's qualifications. He founded two monasteries near Marseilles – St Victor for men and Holy Saviour for women. Cassian wrote *Institutes of the Cenobia*, dedicated to Bishop Castor; later he wrote the *Conferences* in three instalments. Unfortunately, he also became entangled in the semi-Pelagianism of his day, the source of the stigma that tainted his 'official' reputation in the West. Cassian died *c*.435.

Cassian acknowledges some of his sources, but not all. He does not mention the so-called Origenist writings, especially those of Evagrius on whom he relies so heavily. Presumably he wanted to distance himself from the controversy he had encountered in the East. In effect, Cassian interpreted Evagrian spirituality for Western ascetics. The *Institutes* offer a quasi-systematic treatise on cenobitic life among the Egyptian ascetics and how their basic monastic principles may be modified and moderated to Western adaptation. The *Conferences* give the gist of spiritual discussions Cassian and Germanus reputedly had with both anchoritic and cenobitic abbas in Egypt. The *Institutes* make practical assertions; the *Conferences* expound the theological and spiritual dimension underlying the monastic ethos. Along with Athanasius' *Life of Antony*, these two works tell us most of what we know about primitive monasticism.[21] The question of solitude was very important to Cassian, especially when trying to adapt monastic spirituality to fifth-century Gaul.

Cassian extolled the anchorites he met in Egypt. He was amazed and awed by them. It would be difficult to miss his bias toward eremitism – standing as an ideal, even if one largely unattainable in the West. Typically, he points out the eremitical 'superiority': how the eremitical is more sublime than cenobitic life because the contemplation of God is so much more important than the active communal life; how the monks in the great wilderness, away from all companionship, possess spiritual enlightenment.[22] And again, the hermits are those fighting an open battle with the demons, unafraid to imitate John the Baptist, Elijah, Elisha and the other prophets.[23]

Desert spirituality is alive in John Cassian, but he is not oblivious to the dangers of desert solitude, nor the problems posed by faulty solitude. As the desert filled up with hermits, solitude became harder to find. Many who had no monastic experience or direction proved problematic for those trying to live the authentic vocation. Other 'false' solitaries were simply misanthropes and charlatans, fleeing human society. Cassian cautions against too precipitous an experience of solitude: if the monk has not done his ascetical homework and rooted out beforehand the vices plaguing him, then he will have to fight them again in solitude.[24] He points out the 'surer' (if not the more sublime) way of the cenobium, with all the strengths that communal life, discipline, direction and accountability bring.

For Cassian, the would-be monk must renounce the world. True to the desert tradition, he stressed separation. Anchorites living in areas where only a few ascetics dwelled had edified Germanus and Cassian. How hard they worked to exist in their love of solitude with God![25] Here the spirituality of the cell played an important role of stability and perseverance. Continual prayer and the contemplation of God are fruits of solitude and perseverance. Contemplation, only attainable in solitude,[26] is a gift for those who have assiduously done the required inner work.

One finds little mention of Cassian outside monastic circles. The Roman Church never canonised him and many grew suspicious of his work. Cassian's spiritual message is concerned with the encounter between an individual soul and God – spirituality via the Egyptian desert. He interpreted its wisdom for Western monastics. The Church in the East, however, did canonise him. And the Church of Marseilles celebrates him, as do monasteries in the West. Pope Urban V even attributed to him the title 'saint'. Still, he remains elusive and largely unknown in the West. Even so, one can discern Cassian's influence in the individualism of devotional medieval piety. And though the direct influence of Cassian is seen in later Western monastic rules (e.g. those of Caesarius, the Master and Benedict) and in the eleventh-century reform traditions of Romuald, Peter Damian and Bruno, as well as monastic spirituality throughout the centuries, his more indirect line of influence would be felt to a limited extent in various ascetical writings – even outside the monastic ethos. And anyone concerned with monastic solitude throughout the centuries has been deeply indebted to John Cassian.

THEODORET OF CYR

When we move to Syria on the monastic map, it is difficult not to smile. Unfortunately, the ascetical extremes and outright aberrations of the area have monopolised history's focus, to the detriment of all those early Syrian monastics whose authentic vocation and monastic witness almost disappear in the mix. Those *boskoi* who grazed on grass and roots like cattle, the 'statics' who might have spent their lives only in a standing position – covered with heavy chains – the *akoimetoi* who lived without sleep, or the 'stylites' who remained atop pillars or towers unto death: these could easily garner the lion's share of attention, even today.

We do not know the exact origins of Syrian monasticism,

whether it developed largely under the influence of Egypt, uniquely on its own concurrently with Egyptian monasticism, highly influenced by Mesopotamian dualism, or all of the above. Syrian monasticism was different from its Egyptian counterpart, even on the physical plane. There was more water in the Syrian steppes/desert than in Egypt, for one thing. The Syrian brand certainly had its similarities with Egyptian monasticism: anchorites and cenobites, male and female. But when it came to ascetical feats, Syria ruled the day.

Theodoret of Cyr – monk and bishop – was both a supporter of monasticism and an advocate for the holiness of all people. When Theodoret wrote about Syrian monks, he did so to encourage others to model their lives on the virtues embraced by the monks. The anchorites lived the virtues to a heroic degree, so they became Theodoret's immediate focus, on behalf of society. The popular devotion towards these ascetics helped to fashion Syrian ideas about holiness and perfection. The Syrian saints distanced themselves from family, friends, money and food, indeed from all 'normal' and 'human' realities. Having distanced themselves from society, they became the interveners in history who could be passionless and objective seers and savants.

Theodoret was born at Antioch in 393 of wealthy Christian parents. He joined the monastery after pursuing his education. In 423 he became Bishop of Cyr. He knew both Syriac and Greek, enabling him to converse with the various monastic ascetics of his day, as well as to write learned works of apologetical, exegetical and historical competence. The work of interest to the world of solitude is his *History of the Monks of Syria* (variously, *Religious History*, *Ascetic Life*, *Philothée History*) in which Theodoret offered the witness of 30 primary ascetics and their followers for people to admire, venerate and even imitate – within reason. He presented them as true athletes in the Christian arena, people who went to extremes to conquer their desires and thoughts, but never forced others to live likewise. They dwelt in cages, covered themselves in heavy chains, and lived year-round under open skies, doing without adequate food, water, clothing or shelter. They each seemed to add a unique personal ingredient to the ascetical mix, so that one could (without knowing historical factors) assume that fourth- and fifth-century Syria must have appeared to some a rather appalling three-ring circus.

But evidently Theodoret proved a moderating force among the ascetics. He wrote of encouraging moderation – cajoling, suggesting, and occasionally ordering by episcopal authority, the cessation of ascetical extremes. At times, he seemed divided within himself; he admired their ascetical feats and disapproved fanatical excess. Theodoret described them as living the 'angelic life' here on earth by renouncing marriage, controlling their bodies and minds, and maintaining constant prayer. This 'angelic life' speaks to an underlying dualism that considered bodily existence something negative, at best, as if the solitaries were living in the 'Spirit' while the rest of humanity existed in the flesh. The ascetics emulated the desert prophets: Moses, Elijah, Elisha and John the Baptist. Like those prophets, individual ascetics would leave their solitude from time to time to denounce heresy and civil unrest. Others left it permanently to minister as priests and bishops (like Theodoret himself).

Syrian monasticism considered solitude the pinnacle of life. As with part of the Egyptian desert movement, Syrians viewed the cenobium in a less favourable light than the anchorite's cave, hole in the ground, cage or tower. The monk Eusebius' opinion would have been typical – pray for salvation anywhere you can find some solitude.[27] Theodoret's spirituality was, of course, monastic spirituality and as such, solitude was held the ideal for all to imitate. Here was a spirituality whose ideal was urged upon everyone, even if its more extreme embodiments seemed to breathe a rarer air than most other Christian believers. Theodoret's own voice called for moderation, charity, interior peace and balance.

CYRIL OF SCYTHOPOLIS

Theodoret's monastic history of Syria found a place in the library of a monk in Palestine who, in turn, wrote the lives of early Palestinian monks – Cyril of Scythopolis. He was born *c.*525 in Scythopolis to pious parents who took active roles in Palestinian church life. St Sabas knew Cyril's family well, even to the point of staying with them when on ecclesiastical business in the area. Sabas nurtured Cyril's monastic vocation from childhood, and Cyril entered monastic life as soon as he could, in 543 under George of Beella who became his friend and advisor. Cyril's other great mentor was John the Solitary (the 'Hesychast') whose life Cyril included in his work, *Lives of the Monks of Palestine*. Although the exact date of his death is uncertain, Cyril seems to have died in his mid-thirties *c.*560.

Monastic historians deeply appreciate Cyril's painstaking scholarship and overall sense of history. With Cyril, monastic hagiography took a major step forward. Along with bio-graphical and geographical details, as well as descriptions of miracles, Cyril situates his biographies within dated political and ecclesiastical parameters – years, rulers, church councils, etc. After a massive task of note-taking and interviewing elder monks, he retold the stories of the founders of Palestinian monasticism and noted details that set Palestinian apart from Egyptian and Syrian monastic life. Cyril's 'Lives' of Euthymius and Sabas form the first part of the work, followed by the 'Life of John the Hesychast' and four other monks.

Whereas Egyptian monasticism developed on the fringes of extreme desert (yet close enough to the Nile for water), and Syrian monasticism emerged in the mountains where pools of water collected in rocks and vegetation prospered, Palestinian monasticism developed chiefly in a surprisingly small area where three continents and their distinctive soils meet.[28] The hills of Judaea are Mediterranean; the Dead Sea valley is an arm of the Great Rift of Africa; between them lay Asian steppes. Cyril studied the monasteries that developed in this strip of land where monks could gather rain water and, occasionally, spring water into cisterns and reservoirs through canal systems. They grew garden vegetables, collected wild vegetation, purchased food from local markets, and accepted donated goods.

An earlier Palestinian monasticism had existed under Chariton, whom Chitty calls 'the protomonk' of the Judaean desert.[29] Chariton developed an early system of 'laura' life, using a series of individual cells or caves clustered around a central area for common worship and assembly. But the real founder of the type of monasticism that thrived in the Judaean wilderness was Euthymius. When he came to the Jerusalem area in 405, he learned what he could about monastic life from the monks already there, at Pharan. He and his friend Theoctistus then became hermits in a cave. Soon a community formed around them. Euthymius lived on the communal fringe, joining the others on Sundays. A lover of silence and solitude, he jealously guarded his withdrawal, refusing all contact with outsiders – both secular and ecclesial. His monasteries, based on Chariton's laura of Pharan, became a movement, with Euthymius as spiritual abba. He began a custom of moving into the 'utter desert' (called *Rouba* by the monks) for a Lenten retreat running from late January until Palm Sunday. Euthymius considered this retreat as following the example of Elijah and John the Baptist.

Cyril's second 'life' treats Sabas who founded in 483 the Great Laura (called *Mar-Saba* today), ten years after Euthymius' death. This laura is still populated today. Another lover of solitude, Sabas applied himself to solitude, fasting and ceaseless prayer.[30] Unlike Euthymius, Sabas entered the fray of ecclesiastical politics. He visited church leaders regularly; served as legate; attended councils and the court of Justinian; founded hospices in Jerusalem, both for his own monks and for visiting monks from abroad; and established seven lauras. Some of these latter foundations resulted from the Lenten solitude retreat he continued after his predecessor's death. In late 492, the desert monks addressed the Patriarch of Jerusalem, asking that Sabas and Theodosius be named archimandrites of the lauras and anchorites (Sabas) and the cenobia (Theodosius).

Palestinian monasticism developed as a blend of racial, religious and cultural traditions, including the local Arab population, many of whom became Christian through their dealings with the monks. Some of these eventually joined the monastic ranks and even became leaders within the movement. Hirschfeld[31] asserts there were at least 19 lauras in the Judaean desert during these years. Cenobia developed to serve the needs of newcomers who could not cope with the stark solitude and independent lifestyle in the lauras. The monks of Palestine grew strong bonds with the Jerusalem Church and were not at all passive in local ecclesial politics. The Palestinian Church itself fostered an ascetical and monastic spirituality. It is a bit ironic to discover these fierce solitaries from arid wilderness at the very hub of the Palestinian Church. Their influence is felt in the Orthodox Church's liturgical and ascetical spiritualities that they helped form.

JOHN CLIMACUS

John Climacus (variously John the Scholastic and John of the Ladder) lived on Mount Sinai in the late sixth and early seventh centuries. When he was sixteen, he placed himself under an ascetic named Martyrius who tonsured John atop Mount Sinai three years later. Both John the Sabbaite and Abbot Anastasius of Sinai are reported to have recognised a future abbot of Sinai in the young monk. Martyrius soon died and John became a hermit at Tholas, some five miles distant from the main monastery. Before long, monks recognised John as a spiritual father and began turning to him for spiritual direction. At some point during the forty years he spent as a hermit at Tholas, John journeyed to Egypt, spending some time at a large cenobium close to Alexandria. To his dismay, the monks of Sinai elected him abbot. During his abbacy he wrote *The Ladder of Divine Ascent* at the request of Abbot John of Raithu, a neighbouring monastery on the Gulf of

Suez. John Climacus' biographer, Daniel of Raithu, also came from this nearby monastery. Abbot John Climacus resigned shortly before his death, so he could taste again the delights of solitude.

The *Ladder* is a work intended for monks and, although non-monks should benefit from its reading, the work's monastic spirituality is always unmistakably present. The *Ladder* treats monastic virtues and vices, often describing with evident humour and irony the problems encountered on the monastic journey. Here was a hermit writing for cenobites. John Climacus used a number of sources available to him, including the Scriptures, *The Sayings of the Desert Fathers*, Evagrius Ponticus, and John Cassian (under the name Nilus). Abbot John's preference for monastic life rested between the poles of strictly anchoritic solitude and cenobitic monasticism. The middle way – living solitude in a small grouping under a spiritual father – combines the two. Echoing Euthymius in Palestine – and many others before him – John Climacus advised that no one should jump into solitude unless they have learned how to live with others in community, or in the 'middle' way. He stressed that solitude is certainly not intended for the angry monk, but even for those who might peacefully live a solitary life, the dangers of vainglory, pride and *acedia* are a lifelong threat. One of John's colourful illustrations about solitude relates how he overheard nearby solitaries raging alone like caged birds in their cells; he advised them to leave the solitary life before they turned into devils.[32] Climacus encouraged solitude for those who could live it healthily, always under a spiritual director.

Silence is the language of communion with God. For monks in community, wrote Climacus, it is an antidote to anger. Quieting the emotions and thoughts lead to that calm and tranquillity – that *hesychia* – that utters the true prayer of love. In his remarkably helpful introduction to the *Ladder*, Kallistos Ware stresses that stillness not only reflects the solitary at peace in the cell, but also a propensity for ceaseless prayer.[33] And there, once again, we are at the crux of monastic spirituality – unceasing, continual prayer. As a path towards that goal, Sinaitic spirituality has markedly influenced the course of Orthodox monasticism and spirituality, as well as countless Western monastics and spiritual seekers. Climacus' *Ladder* is a Christian classic that has withstood countless generations of monastic strife and cultural change.

ISAAC OF NINEVEH

Isaac of Nineveh would also use the 'ladder' image to signify the spiritual journey. Dive down deeply, he wrote, and you will discover the ladder's steps on which you can ascend to the Kingdom of God.[34] Little is known about the life of this enigmatic mystic of seventh-century Mesopotamia. We know he was born in Qatar on the Persian Gulf and became a monk in what is now northern Iraq. Shortly after his area was brought back into union with Syria following a period of thirty schismatic years, Isaac became Bishop of Nineveh. A new 'Nestorian' bishop could not have been very palatable to the Jacobites of Nineveh, and perhaps this fact proved persuasive in Isaac's decision to resign his see after only five months. He joined a group of hermits on Mount Matout in Huzistan and, later, lived with the monks of Rabban Shabur monastery in present-day Iran until his death as a very old, blind solitary.[35] Once blind, he dictated his works to his disciples in the Shabur monastery, who called him, in reference to the famous Didymus the Blind, Didymus II.[36]

Through Evagrius, Isaac brought Origenist views into his spirituality, not surprisingly since the Syrians blithely handed down the Evagrian tradition under his own name, generation after generation. Isaac was a solitary writing to solitaries about solitude. Even so, much of his writing is quite applicable to ordinary Christian living, enjoying popularity through translations into at least fourteen languages. One interesting note: monks of St Sabas' monastery made the original Greek translation in ninth-century Palestine, although St Sabas had been the arch-foe of the Palestinian Origenist monks. Unwittingly, St Sabas allowed Evagrius re-entry into Palestine.[37]

Again, Isaac was writing for solitaries. Isaac's hero is *ihidaya*, the 'solitary one', or literally, 'single one'.[38] But in the Syrian tradition, this can mean one who is single-minded, centred on God alone and following a path of conversion in silence. Keeping silence is like watering the plants of inner growth towards spiritual knowledge.[39] Solitude is an absolute for this journey; through it one can experience union with God. By separating from the world, one strives in solitude to reach a state of stillness where union can happen. Solitaries must heal their own souls before healing others. What should one do in solitude? Fast, pray, keep night vigils, perform prostrations day and night.[40]

If one experiences darkness in solitude – and Isaac assures the solitary that darkness will certainly come – the remedy is the same as in Egypt or Syria or Palestine: patient endurance. There is room for slipping and failure, but not for despair. Isaac prescribed daily conversion for all. With patient endurance in silent solitude, we can attain love of God. And in love of God, the love of neighbour is born in stillness and peace. We often find in the world of mysticism this image: a simple heart reaching out to the universe in love. This universality of scope and inclusiveness of humanity seems, somehow, inevitable. Isaac's experience was that, if you find yourself feeling compassion for all of humanity without any prejudice or distinction, and your heart is afire with love, then you are at peace.[41] What a beautiful vision! What an enviable place to be! If only the world could be lit with this kind of luminosity!

PART THREE: CORPORATE SOLITUDE

7. SOLITUDE IN BENEDICT OF NURSIA

Gregory the Great was a capable statesman, pre-eminent pontiff and prolific writer during the second half of the sixth century. In his *Dialogues*, Gregory contributed hagiographical materials about several holy people of that age, not the least of whom was Benedict of Nursia, treated in book two of the *Dialogues*. Other than the *Benedictine Rule*, it is only through the *Dialogues* that we read anything substantial about the 'father' of Western monasticism. At the end of book two, Gregory recommends to the reader the reading of this *Rule*. This helped to advertise and circulate the *Rule* beyond the monastic circles where it had already spread. At this stage of monastic history – even though we have taken a slight step back chronologically from Isaac to Benedict – it is not surprising to read Gregory describing Benedict in terms of patriarchs and prophets (e.g. Moses, Elijah, Elisha, David, Christ). Not only is this consonant with earlier primary monastic sources, but also a good hagiographical technique in Gregory's day. A primary guide for the *Dialogues* will be found in Sulpicius Severus' *Life of St Martin* (of Tours), but the *Apophthegmata* and *Life of Antony* also served Gregory well in the fashioning of Benedict's life.

Benedict was born *c*.480 in the area of Nursia. As a youth he travelled to Rome for an education, but was so distressed by Roman morals that he fled to a place called Effide and went into the 'desert' wilderness to live as a hermit at Subiaco, 46 miles from Rome. After an aborted attempt as abbot of a nearby monastery, Benedict returned to his solitude where his reputation grew and followers joined him. He built a number of monasteries in the vicinity to accommodate all these monks and became essentially the head of a small monastic congregation. Leaving Subiaco when local jealousy reared its head, Benedict and a few disciples then moved to Monte Cassino where they built a monastery over the ruins of a pagan temple to Apollo. Benedict died there *c.*547, having written the *Rule* and watched his cenobitic flock flourish.

Oddly, Benedict had no actual introduction to monastic life. When he left Effide, Benedict met on the road a monk named Romanus. Instead of joining Romanus and becoming a monk at his monastery under the rule of Adeodatus, Benedict instead received a habit from Romanus and began his eremitical life at Subiaco. Only Romanus in his nearby monastery knew the arrangement. So Benedict began his ascetical life alone, without any cenobitic training or spiritual guide. Fortunately for Benedict, Romanus at least smuggled bread to him periodically, dropping it by rope down the cliff face to Benedict's cave. Clearly, Benedict had withdrawn from the world for a life of solitude, 'learnedly ignorant and wisely unskilled', as Gregory put it.[1] He lived as had the desert ascetics of old. The story of Benedict, caught in the throes of sensual temptation and throwing his naked body into thorns and nettles as an antidote, could have been written of an Egyptian abba. While he was still a young hermit, others began seeking Benedict out, including the monks of a nearby monastery, who made him their abbot, then later tried to poison him because he was so austere. Eventually, a community formed around him in solitude.

Benedict left the monastic world his legacy in the *Rule*. He relied heavily upon the anonymous *Rule of the Master* for the composition of his own monastic legislation. Since the *Rule of the Master* depends significantly upon John Cassian's *Conferences*, Benedict too exhibits signs of Cassian in his *Rule*. But Benedict did not hesitate to moderate the harshness and verbosity of the *Rule of the Master* when he wrote for his own monks. Benedict repeats Cassian and the Master's respect for hermits in his first chapter ('On the Kinds of Monks') but he quickly focuses the entire *Rule* on the cenobitic life, even though the *Rule of the Master* and Cassian treat both kinds of monastic life as progressive stages. Benedict does not again mention hermits.

Besides Cassian and the *Rule of the Master*, Basil's monastic writings also played a part in the formulation of the *Rule*. Benedict does not echo Basil's condemnation of the hermit life, even if his own accent fixes entirely on cenobitic life. We know that Basil's writings strongly influenced the development of Western monasticism. Benedict himself recommends them in his *Rule*, but he quietly departs from Basil on the question of hermits. Given his personal experience of eremitical life without the benefit of cenobitic training, Benedict allows for hermits, but only after years of communal life. He knew personally the dangers and hardships of solitary life, but he also recognised the validity of hermit life after years of community experience. What does Benedict, who arguably has had the most formative influence on Western monasticism, have to say about solitude? Very little, actually. Clearly, he had his own solitary experience. Then he opened his heart to those who came to him seeking the ways of God. Forming them into communal life, he had to find a way to make solitude possible in the midst of community. The rules for the language of silence in the *Rule* try to effect that provision.

Benedict dotted his *Rule* with mentions of silence, but also devoted an entire chapter (#6) to the observance of silence – placing it between chapters on obedience and humility. To create an atmosphere of silence in the Benedictine community is crucial – an atmosphere within which every monk or nun can do the 'work' of solitude, maintaining a mindfulness of divine presence. By cultivating this silence – providing one another with the ability to listen more clearly and attentively – Benedict's followers help to create, in effect, solitude within communal life. Benedictines form community to experience solitude together. And silence is the language of solitude for listening hearts, readying those listeners to ponder God's Word in Scripture, prayer and communal life. Silence, for Benedict, maintains an awareness of God's presence. To enable others around oneself to do so, it is important not to disturb others. The *Rule* regulates silence to promote contemplative union and communion. For those who can sustain solitude and silence, contemplation is a possibility and communion, a gift.

Of the many Western monastic rules developed before and after Benedict of Nursia, the *Rule* flourished the most and spread during ensuing centuries. When Charlemagne adopted it for his Empire – championed by Benedict of Aniane – its primacy was assured. Anchorites continued to exist, often attaching themselves to Benedictine monasteries and placing themselves under Benedictine abbots and priors. Many Benedictines became recluses at the end of their lives. Peter Anson states that this was not an uncommon part of Benedictine monasticism before AD 1000.[2] Other solitaries tended to live in forests not far from cenobitic foundations. Even today, the occasional monastery or abbey will number among its members a hermit living somewhere on the property, either temporarily or in permanent reclusion.

But because clear provisions for solitaries were made neither by the *Rule* nor by the general monastic world, the question of solitude suffered its ups and downs through medieval times. From the eleventh century onwards, successful eremitic movements sprang up and offered solitaries the canonical standing to live their vocation within the established ecclesial order. Turning towards greater silence and solitude in the name of contemplation's call, groups like the Camaldolese, Avellaniti, Vallombrosans, Cistercians, Olivetans, Celestines, Grandmontines and Carthusians flourished. Interestingly, all but the two latter groups adopted the *Benedictine Rule* as their rule of life, though within a framework favouring solitude. Occasionally, a voice would rise to cast a 'Basilian' stone at the very idea of hermits, so that historical opinion tended to fluctuate between a respect for eremitical life and a general distrust of hermits (or fear of solitary excess). As cenobites tended to assume more active apostolates, they, in turn, would receive the criticism (sometimes scorn) of hermits who accused them of diluting the possibilities for monastic solitude and silence. Tensions have existed between hermits and cenobites over the question of solitude. At times, the rhetoric would become, unfortunately, vitriolic. Two different paths – each clinging to its emphasis – would argue about their shared monastic call.

8. CAMALDOLESE BENEDICTINE SOLITUDE: THE LAURA[1]

It seems almost tautological to mention 'Camaldoli' and 'solitude' within the same sentence, since solitude has been such a hallmark of Camaldolese tradition from its inception. Fulfilling a distinct need within the monastic world, Camaldolese solitude became the historical springboard for the growth of its congregation and has formed a mainstay of Camaldolese spirituality throughout its first millennium of existence.

ROMUALD OF RAVENNA

What we substantively know of Romuald's life and ministry can be found in Peter Damian's *Life of Blessed Romuald* and Bruno-Boniface of Querfurt's *Life of the Five Brothers*. In the latter work we find reference to Otto III's threefold good suggested to Romuald and his followers, the second advantage being 'golden solitude, for those who are mature and who thirst for the living God'.[2] Otto was urging Romuald and his followers to send a group on a mission to Poland where they could experience cenobitic life, eremitism and quite possibly martyrdom (the third 'good'). Romuald, who devoted most of his life to monastic solitude, organising hermits to live in community, founding hermitages and monasteries, as well as reforming already extant monastic houses, was at least tacitly compliant with Otto's monastic schema vis-à-vis Poland, but continued to live his own vocation to 'golden solitude' in an exemplary fashion for at least protracted periods of several years, alternating with various itinerant journeys concerned with founding and reforming monastic groups. Peter Damian's biography of the hermit indicates Romuald's wanderlust, as he was always eager to make new foundations. Bruno-Boniface corroborates this view: 'Abbot Romuald – always a wanderer, now here, now there, gathering disciples . . .'[3]

Peter Damian relates that Romuald already experienced solitude's call as a young man in the forest. He became a monk at the newly 'Cluniacised' abbey of St Apollinare in Classe near Ravenna, but left after a few years of frustration with his fellow monks' lack of fervour and, with permission of his abbot, began to live as the disciple of a hermit named Marino in the Ravenna countryside. After they had moved to the Abbey of St Michael of Cuxa (a successfully 'Cluniacised' house), this same duo built a hermitage close to the abbey, but the roles of master and disciple were now reversed. Soon other disciples joined them and the little group studied monastic sources and performed their ascesis. It is instructive to read Romuald's teaching from these idyllic years near Cuxa, sensing in his wisdom why he quickly became known as a spiritual master for solitaries.

> Be constant in your practice, and one day He who gave you the desire for the prayer of the heart will give you that prayer itself. When your heart's intention is fixed on God, it will keep lit the incense of your prayer, and the wind of distraction will not put it out. Do not worry about stray thoughts; they may come and go, but they will not take your attention away from God.[4]

Romuald was single-minded and went about his life's work of engendering monastic solitude and bringing solitaries wholeheartedly together into community.

Romuald's unique vocation seemed to vacillate between periods of relative seclusion or reclusion and those times when he felt impelled to journey forth in founding and reforming activities. Jean Leclercq viewed the years of reclusion as underpinning all Romuald's activities.[5] Solitude certainly was central to Romuald's spirituality. Unfortunately, we suffer the paucity of documentation regarding his spiritual teachings. As with many great mystics throughout the centuries, we must rely on what few accounts of Romuald's life and testament form the tradition of his teaching on solitude. Peter Damian indicates that mindfulness in solitary prayer was central to Romuald: 'Better to sing one psalm with feeling... than to recite a hundred with a wandering mind.'[6] From Bruno-Boniface we have what has been called the 'Brief Rule' of Romuald:

> Sit in your cell as in paradise. Put the whole world behind you and forget it. Watch your thoughts like a good fisherman watching for fish. The path you must follow is in the Psalms – never leave it... Realize above all that you are in God's presence... Empty yourself completely and sit waiting, content with the grace of God.[7]

For Romuald, solitude accords the possibility to commune with God, to speak with God. The grace derived from this living relationship enabled Romuald to journey forth from solitude quite literally, to bring to fruition his own spiritual freedom and immense love of God. This freedom expressed itself in many ways, so that his works of monastic foundation and reformation were not restricted to one model or type of being monastic.

PETER DAMIAN OF FONTE AVELLANA

Romuald's biographer not only champions the memory of a holy hermit given to wandering, reforming, and itinerant preaching; he also embraces the founder's great passion for solitude and propagating sanctuaries for living that solitude. Like his predecessor, Peter Damian also became quite the monastic founder and reformer in his own right. And like Romuald, Peter Damian also founded cenobitic and eremitical houses without undue prejudice towards a set form that those houses might take. But again, the biographer's own preference is for solitude and the eremitical life. True to Western monastic culture, Peter Damian centres on purity of heart in his praise of eremitism.[8] To keep that heart pure, the hermit must be able to enjoy certain conditions of life that will be constant and familiar companions – an atmosphere of quiet, the maintenance of silence; the asceticism of fasting. All three of these external conditions must be tempered with the traditional monastic virtues of moderation and discretion.

Probably the most popularly known work by Peter Damian is his Opus XI, the so-called *The Lord Be with You*, with its ruminations about solitude, the eremitical life, and the relationship between hermit and Church. The point of departure is the query about the propriety of a hermit-priest who celebrates Eucharist alone responding to the words: 'The Lord be with you'. This immediately brings into question the hermit's relationship to the greater Church. For Peter Damian, the solitary represents the Church; the Church subsists in the person of the hermit.[9]

His ecclesiology is sound, even if the air in Peter Damian's cell seems a bit rarefied. The Church is present in each individual member of the mystical body; each member is substantially the Church that is one in all. Dedicated solitude within the Church is also a collective act; solitude is plural, while community is singular.[10] By love, the entire Church is present in the hermit. André Louf calls this 'corporate' solitude[11] because the hermit is united to all in the Holy Spirit. True to Romuald, his mentor, Peter Damian calls the cell 'paradise' and enlists a number of metaphors to describe its qualities. It is a school where the heavenly arts are taught; a mirror of souls where self-knowledge leads to spiritual growth; a bridal chamber leading to contemplative union; a fountain of life; a haven and refuge nursing the soul to health.

But the cell is not only paradise; it forms a crossroads between heaven and earth. Since it is a meeting place, solitude is also a purgatory; a furnace or kiln or workshop wherein the work of perfection is fashioned, moulded, and brought into being; a bath that cleanses, purifies and shines. The solitary's way is a road of return to God, on whose path one travels through the desert wastes of the heart. However, the cell's activities can often move from purgatorial struggles into the full combat of an inferno in the spiritual arena. So, solitude is also a real battlefield, sometimes a bloody one. And at times, the solitary cell will become a tomb where reality comes to light and life in the power of the Spirit. Paradise, purgatory, inferno – solitude's cell is all this and more for Peter Damian. Eremitical solitude seems to many to have more than a tinge of individualism about it, but for Romuald and Peter Damian, the community bonds of obedience and communion protect the solitary from individualistic pursuits. Still, when reading Peter Damian, one can sense the individual coming to the fore between the lines of the text. But even if he has a strong individualistic strain running through his writings, Peter Damian is deeply concerned that the hermit is intentionally part of the Church and intimately concerned with church life. Solitude is meant to foster love for and within the church communion.

RUDOLF OF CAMALDOLI

Rudolf, fourth prior of Camaldoli, wrote his *Constitutions* in 1080, producing a shorter version in 1085. These *Constitutions* really form more of a customary wherein Rudolf describes life as it was lived at eleventh-century Camaldoli. They are not a list of rules and restrictions, but of customs and descriptions. Naturally, the early founders of Camaldoli developed a spirituality of the cell consonant with Romuald's teaching in the 'Brief Rule'. The monastic cell was the place of grace and solitude. 'Let the solitary cultivate a continual and perpetual fidelity to the cell, so that through the grace of God and his assiduous stability, living in the cell will become sweet to him.'[12] But from their humble beginnings as hermits in the Romualdian mould and then down through the Camaldolese centuries, the monks did not let the cell of solitude detract from the communal aspects of their monastic life. If the solitary's life seemed busy to an outsider, it was meant to be so. 'Everyone ought to be so diligent either in prayer, reading, or performing disciplines, prostrations and flagellations, that the whole space of a day and night seems brief and insufficient to him.'[13]

Rudolf's solitary cell is also a spiritual arena for the development of various virtues. Romuald consistently encouraged hermits to place themselves under obedience to live the monastic virtue of *discretio* (discretion). Rudolf insists that obedience 'is very necessary to solitaries, and, since they lead a harder life, they should observe a fuller obedience'.[14] And of course, moderation should not be lacking at Camaldoli: 'Sobriety . . . ought to be applied to all our actions so that eating, fasting, keeping vigil, sleeping, standing, walking, speaking, keeping silence and all our other actions be performed soberly and moderately.'[15] But perhaps the virtue that speaks most significantly in Rudolf is piety, which he equates with kindness and gentleness. 'Piety is also very necessary to solitaries, so that they may be humane, kind, merciful and meek. Piety is a kind inclination of the heart, bending with merciful humanity to another's infirmity.'[16] We may be tempted to think that eleventh-century hermits might have been a bit gruff, introverted and fiercely focused, as they lived the hard rigours of Camaldoli. Rudolf's comments speak more to the bonds of love that characterised the Romualdian world where the 'privilege of love' was of the utmost importance.[17]

PAUL GIUSTINIANI OF MONTE CORONA

Thomas Giustiniani was born a noble in Venice in 1476. He enjoyed a humanist education in Venice, at the University of Padua and on the island of Murano in the Venetian lagoon. A devotee of Stoic philosophy, Giustiniani renounced physical pleasure and, after undertaking a trip to the Holy Land, joined the Camaldolese in 1510 at the Holy Hermitage of Camaldoli. Peter Quirini, another Venetian nobleman, followed him there and both soon became involved with reform work of the Camaldolese Order. In 1513 their friend John di Medici was elected pope and, as Leo X, helped the newly professed hermits with their reform work. Giustiniani (now Paul) became superior at the Holy Hermitage in 1516 and, four years later, published at Camaldoli his *Rule of the Eremitical Life*. Because his reform work was such a discouragingly uphill battle and thankless task at Camaldoli where the majority were not then reform-minded, Giustiniani gradually focused his efforts on forming an eremitical group of like-minded hermits outside Camaldoli. Although he was re-elected Camaldoli's superior, Giustiniani left the Holy Hermitage in the fall of 1520 (with Leo X's blessing) and began to live the hermit life in the Italian Marches. When disciples began to gather, a new eremitical institute – The Company of Hermits of St Romuald (later Camaldolese Hermits of Monte Corona) – began in 1523 with five hermitages. After becoming autonomous in 1525, this Congregation began to grow and expand. Bl. Paul Giustiniani died in 1528.

The major portion of Giustiniani's twelve volumes of work remains unpublished. Almost all his writings are geared to eremitical life and spirituality. His sources: the Camaldolese *Constitutions* of Bl. Rudolf and Gerard; Peter Damian; *Lives* and *Sayings* of the desert tradition; Cassian; the *Benedictine Rule*; the Cappadocians; Jerome; Augustine; Gregory the Great; Bernard and William of St-Thierry. Giustiniani based his own hermitages on the laura-style monasticism of Camaldoli and the much earlier Palestinian monasticism. He wanted them located in wilderness areas. The cells – like a laura – would each be separate so every hermit had the freedom to read, sing and pray aloud without disturbing others.[18] Solitude was absolute to Giustiniani. Hermits must guard the solitude above all else.[19] One might call Giustiniani a solitary of solitaries; at times he may even seem obsessed with solitude. He certainly was its champion. In some ways, his life became a work of solitude. He likened it to a door through which the Holy Spirit enters the soul.

Giustiniani called silence the primary adornment of solitude.[20] Though the young must be particularly vigilant about it during their first years of eremitical life, all the hermits, and especially the recluses, were to observe an unbreakable silence always.[21] That way, ceaseless prayer and meditation in monastic life could be safeguarded. There would be no cenobitic dimension to Giustiniani's movement. The hermits were to pray always – by reading, meditating, vocal prayer, studying, manual labour – as long as they kept the profound peace of solitude.[22] The founder felt called to restore the original eremitical work of Romuald. The Monte Corona Congregation still exists, carrying on Paul Giustiniani's 'work' of solitude.

ANSELM GIABBANI OF CAMALDOLI

Anselm Giabbani was born in 1908 at Papiano di Pratovecchio and entered the Holy Hermitage of Camaldoli in 1923 at the age of fifteen. From his earliest years as a Camaldolese, Giabbani felt drawn to the primary sources of Camaldolese tradition.[23] In 1935 he was appointed prior of Fonte Avellana, where his good friend Benedict Calati served as student-master for all the young monks who accompanied them to the former monastery of Peter Damian. They spent ten years together there – through World War II – where they studied the Camaldolese sources, hagiography and patristic writers, publishing the periodical *Avellana*. Much of their study bore fruit in 1944, with the publication of *Camaldolesi*, a work concerning distinguished Camaldolese in history. In 1945 Giabbani published *L'Eremo*, a study of Camaldolese sources and spirituality. He then became the Procurator General for the Order in Rome. This 'was an ideal place from which to realize his long-standing dream: to renew, in the most official way possible, the "Constitutions" of the Camaldolese Hermit monks and place Camaldoli finally in the modern stream'.[24] He was instrumental in the publication of the monastic journal *Camaldoli* (later changed to *Vita Monastica*). After Giabbani became Prior General in 1951, he continued to promote the study and publication of Camaldolese sources in Italian, as well as the renewal of the 'Constitutions'.

Like Giustiniani, Giabbani was a champion of the hermit life, but differed from the humanist solitary on the question of monastic formation. Giabbani defended rigorously the place of solitude in the Church and was unafraid to enter the polemical fray on eremitical spirituality's behalf – including the Camaldolese institution of reclusion. But he saw the Camaldolese cenobium and hermitage as 'the two moments of the same monastic life and thereby preserving the unity of the monk's spiritual course'.[25] The cenobitic life is important and necessary for monastic formation. The hermit's solitude and silence of the cell is a beautiful reality for those who have been prepared by the cenobitic 'rubbing of shoulders'. Camaldolese life is akin to the Palestinian monasticism of Saba and Euthymius.

Giabbani does not lessen the importance of Camaldolese solitude; in fact, he sees it as a higher part of monastic progression. 'There are three stages: from the world to the cenobium; from the cenobium to the hermitage; and from the hermitage to total union with God.'[26] This progression is important to Giabbani. Too many dangers accompany eremitical solitude to allow the unformed, unready, immature and inexperienced to dally in it with romanticised notions and pious dreams. He underlines Camaldolese history, showing that Romuald and Peter Damian erected more cenobitic than eremitical foundations, statistically, all the while favouring the hermit path. For those who are ready for solitude, the silence of life in the Camaldolese 'laura' makes listening to God's Word and uniting with God's presence possible.

Extolled by Romuald and preserved by Peter Damian of Fonte Avellana and the early hermits of Camaldoli, solitude's place was assured in Camaldolese history and spirituality. The Camaldolese way was never a movement away from community and the Church. A distinct part of Romuald's own ministry was to bring isolated hermits and disparate eremitical groups *into* community, under a religious superior. To greater and lesser degrees, Camaldolese hermits and cenobites have espoused solitude as a necessary part of their monastic journey throughout their first millennium of history.

9. CARTHUSIAN SOLITUDE: *ALONE* TOGETHER

Like Romuald and his eleventh-century reform movement, Bruno of Cologne and Rheims had no intention of founding a new religious order. Together with a few like-minded companions, the former diocesan chancellor and cathedral schoolmaster began a rigorous life of solitude in the mountain wilderness near Grenoble, France in 1084. They did so under the juridical protection of Bishop Hugh of Grenoble whose long episcopal reign (1080–1132) allowed this movement that became the Carthusian Order to set down firm roots and develop its *modus vivendi*. In 1090 a former pupil (now Urban II) summoned Bruno to Rome where he served as papal adviser. Later refusing the archbishopric of Reggio, Bruno founded another monastery for solitaries in Calabria (La Torre), where he died in 1101. The Grande Chartreuse in France and La Torre became the springboards for Bruno's movement that stemmed from his love of solitude and contemplation. Though the Order has no 'rule' as such, a series of customaries developed over the years – beginning with those of Guigo I during the 1120s and running down to our own times. These customs, known as the *Statutes* of the Carthusian Order, are basically a combination of Benedictine monasticism and eremitical spirituality (like Camaldolese monasticism) but lived (unlike Camaldolese monasticism) within the context of cells in a monastery, not hermitages.

The Carthusians have always looked directly to the desert monks of early Christianity for their inspiration. Consistently known for their ascetical rigour and uncompromising reputation, Carthusian solitaries have always looked upon their vocation as rare, perhaps even rarer than one might suppose, if questions of mental health and psychological stability are brought into the picture. One Carthusian work admits how hard it is for anyone to maintain his or her psychological balance in ongoing solitude.[1] At some 8,000 feet above sea level in the Alps north of Grenoble, the monks of the motherhouse – the Grande Chartreuse – literally breathe a rarefied air in a rare contemplative atmosphere renowned for its austerity and asceticism. From its onset, the Carthusian Order was not concerned with numbers of members; the *parvus numerus* – small number – designedly set the consistent standard for quality rather than quantity. What was important was that a Carthusian solitary be concerned with waiting upon God, listening to God, and responding to God's presence in courage, honesty, silence and solitude.[2]

Carthusian monasticism differed from the other eremitical reform movements of the eleventh century, such as the Camaldolese and Avellaniti of Peter Damian's Fonte Avellana. They did not consider themselves Benedictines nor drawn to any kind of apostolic work, nor penitential asceticism.[3] But Carthusian solitude is conditioned by the demands of community life – the Divine Office, festal meals and recreational walks. 'The solitude is mitigated by the *cenobitical life*, in such a way that it enjoys the advantages of both [i.e. eremitical and cenobitic] and avoids the disadvantages of living too exclusively separate from one another.'[4] Carthusians are seeking the deepest intimacy with God by their focused solitude. ' "For God Alone" is the Carthusian motto: God alone is their immediate end; to live in union with God as intimately as possible is still their aspiration.'[5] The Carthusian way is unique – much the same in the twenty-first century as it was in the eleventh.

Much of that uniqueness lies in the Carthusian predilection for the solitude of the cell. If the Benedictine aligns stability with a particular community, in a particular monastery or abbey, under a certain abbot or prior, the Carthusian localises stability within the confines of the monastic cell. More than any other religious order, the Carthusians have developed and depend upon a spirituality of the cell. The novice facing commitment knows already by long experience what the boundaries of his desert will be.[6] The Carthusian cell is not only the place of formation, but also the formation director. Solitude in the cell fashions the Carthusian vocation. Carthusians work, eat and sleep in their cells, as well as pray the major portion of the Divine Office there, perform *lectio divina* and study. But dangers lurk in the Carthusian cell, just as they did in fourth-century Egyptian caves and tombs. Solitude of the cell can easily lend itself to fantasy, escape and a plethora of neurotic behaviours. As one Carthusian superior notes, the monk could easily turn his personal little world into the only reality of any consequence, fitting all other factors neatly into an ego-centred world view.[7]

Certainly, there are different approaches one might take towards solitude, even in the Carthusian world. In order for the experience of solitary life to be healthy, one's heart must be pure and the mind open. Solitude as escape or some elaborate response to misanthropy will only invite disaster, probably in short order. Even under the best circumstances, solitude will entail ups and downs, fertility and sterility. Romanticised notions of monastic solitude are not only unhelpful and unproductive, but also dangerously illusory and unhealthy in the context of contemplative life and spirituality. But to live contemplatively in God's presence can be a great grace for those who embrace solitude and silence with authenticity and love. A true solitary will naturally respect the solitude of others. The Carthusian *Statutes* declare that principle early on by asking the monks first to show respect for others' solitude (*Stat.* 1.4.4).[8] This exterior atmosphere of mutual respect will naturally flow from an interior disposition of solitude. Carthusian spirituality sees a necessity for solitude to be 'mitigated by a little common life'.[9] What cenobitic aspects exist in the life of the charterhouse seem so to ensure the health of eremitical solitude.

Solitude in the charterhouse is designedly uncompromising. God's presence is all that matters there. For this 'sharing in the solitude of God' to be authentic, the Carthusian heart aims to be transparent to God in all aspects of contemplative monastic life. But that means that solitude must not be allowed to disintegrate into isolation within community life. One does not enter solitude in order to be dispensed from love's obligations.[10] If solitude is a place for prayer and a viable path to communion, love must be its foundation. The Carthusian solitary's aim, like the foundational aim of other solitaries, is to love and to be in communion with all.[11] True solitaries from all ages have aimed to be united with all, while being separated from all.[12]

Carthusian silence also places an accent on interior openness that allows God entrance. This silence is a means to communication and communion, not an end in itself. Silence is for listening, reflecting and resonating in the heart. This kind of resonation demands a pure heart because communion demands it. To stand in God's presence with heartfelt transparency opens one to a prayerful solidarity with all of creation. Carthusians know themselves as called to this kind of solidarity and communion, in effect a communion of solitude for the world.

GUIGO I OF THE GRANDE CHARTREUSE

Guigo I became the fifth prior of the Grande Chartreuse at the age of twenty-six. The two sources of biographical material on him are the 'Magister Chronicle' of the Carthusian motherhouse and a small portion in the *Life of St Anthelm*. Guigo wrote the famous *Consuetudines Cartusiae*, the *Life of Hugh of Grenoble* (at the behest of Innocent II), the *Meditationes*, and the letter 'On the Solitary Life', in addition to publishing an edition of Jerome's *Letters*. He founded at least six other charterhouses, while overseeing the renovation and restoration of the Grande Chartreuse, as well as the construction of its stone aqueduct. He also developed the library there and maintained correspondence with monastic contemporaries like Bernard and Peter the Venerable. He died in 1136.

Guigo's Carthusian *Consuetudines* (customary) has remained a working document over the centuries, experiencing minor changes, but remaining largely intact. Guigo set the limits for life in a charterhouse: a prior, twelve choir monks, and eighteen *conversi* (lay brothers). His monastic sources were: the *Benedictine Rule*, Cassian, Gregory the Great, the *Apophthegmata*, the *Customs* of Saint-Ruf,[13] Peter Damian's *Avellanita Customary*, and Rudolf of Camaldoli's *Customary*. Guigo's *Meditations* are similar to philosophical musings, but often with the flavour of the apophthegms in their imagery. The anonymous editor of the French edition finds the *Meditations* almost identical to the 'sentences' of Evagrius' *Treatise on Prayer*,[14] though Evagrius' work was unknown in the West at that time. These *Meditations* were often attributed to William of St-Thierry over the centuries. A monastic scholar in the Grenoble library discovered Guigo's letter 'On the Solitary Life' in an old charterhouse manuscript only in 1933. It is a beautiful, enthusiastic endorsement of the Carthusian way of life, encouraging a good friend to join the Grande Chartreuse without delay.

For Carthusians, monastic separation from the world has always been a rigorous, uncompromising form of asceticism. The monastic cell became the centre of focus. For Guigo, the monk needs his cell as a fish needs water.[15] He must stay put in his cell, never leaving it without permission, so as not to disturb others or fritter away time. Guigo considers solitude the place of encounter, as it was for Moses, Elijah, Elisha and John the Baptist. Solitude is necessary for prayer; it is an absolute. Guigo's own description of life in the charterhouse depicts the utmost importance of solitude, so that even liturgy carried less weight.[16]

Silence is an ongoing challenge and must be cultivated continuously. Nothing was more important to the community's life than the silence of solitude.[17] The entire atmosphere of the charterhouse is to promote silence and solitude. That is one reason that, from the beginning, Carthusian life has limited itself to small numbers for each charterhouse.

GUIGO II OF THE GRANDE CHARTREUSE

Guigo II was the ninth prior of the Grand Chartreuse. We know little about him except that he died *c.*1188, after having written *The Ladder of Monks* and *Twelve Meditations* – works ascribed to the pens of others, particularly Bernard of Clairvaux. Surely Guigo's fame was eclipsed by many other Carthusian writers down through the centuries: Denis the Carthusian, Ludolf of Saxony, Surius, Henry Herp, Lanspergius, Guigo du Pont, Pierre Cousturier, Nicholas Kempf, and Hugh of Balma. But Guigo II deserves mention here – albeit brief – because his *Ladder of Monks* influenced countless spiritual writers and movements from the Middle Ages down to present times. He wrote this letter on the contemplative life to Prior Gervase of Mont-Dieu, elaborating on the four stages of classical *lectio divina* as a monastic spiritual exercise, even a monastic *modus vivendi*: reading (*lectio*), meditation (*meditatio*), prayer (*oratio*) and contemplation (*contemplatio*). This process leads predictably to the heart, where the heart's commentary can reveal the inner sense of Scripture.[18] His *Twelve Meditations* offer spiritual and philosophical musings, including some paradoxical ones about monastic solitude and silence.[19]

AUGUSTIN GUILLERAND OF VALSAINTE

Born Maxime Guillerand at Regny-de-Dompierre in 1877, Dom Augustin was ordained a secular priest in 1900. He served as a curate, pastor (twice) and a history professor, before entering the charterhouse of Valsainte in Switzerland at the age of thirty-nine. He had many health problems throughout life, including his years at Valsainte, during which he also seemed to have suffered problems of a psychological nature (e.g. various phobias and a persecution complex). He was known as a 'loner' even among the Carthusians. At Valsainte he lived too much as the man of solitude, to the point of never spending time with the brothers.[20] Guillerand showed a propensity to remain in the solitude of his cell even when he was supposed to be with the community. Finally, in 1928 the General of the Order brought him back to France where he helped out at the liqueur factory in Marseilles for a few months, then served as novice-master at Montrieux. From 1929 to 1935 Guillerand was vicar to the Carthusian nuns near Turin, after which he became prior of the charterhouse in Vedana, Italy and co-visitator for the Italian province. He returned to France from wartime Italy in 1940, when after a brief sojourn at the charterhouse of Sélignac, he joined a small group of Carthusians who, along with their Prior General, were able to reinstall themselves as 'refugees' in their beloved, but abandoned Grande Chartreuse. Augustin Guillerand died there in 1945.

Guillerand has sometimes been referred to as the Carthusian counterpart to Thomas Merton, in the sense that they felt impelled to write and communicate their spiritual journeys – to the great spiritual nourishment of so many. Guillerand's writings were published, anonymously and posthumously: *Carthusian Silence, Carthusian Speech*,[21] *Carthusian Harmony, Facing God, Serene Heights, On the Threshold of the Abyss of God* and other works. Again, like Merton, he had the knack for communicating spirituality to many. Both wrote from the heart of their own experiences, deeply touching the lives of others from their own experiences of silence and solitude. Guillerand's perspective articulated monastic solitude for a twentieth-century spirituality that viewed the world as a place of exile and pilgrim journey.[22]

For Guillerand, separation is simply necessary to the spiritual journey. This journey moves into the depths, beyond all the surface realities distracting us. Nothing matters as much as God's presence and our own union with that presence. Guillerand consistently urges quiet stillness and silent detachment. Perseverance is the door opening to contemplative union; it is a solitary cell. Like Guigo II, Guillerand would sometimes use paradox when speaking of silence and solitude.[23] Silence is a language of union and communion. What Carthusians do *not* say becomes prayer, and that is the best thing they can do.[24] Carthusian life is built upon a profound ground of silence in which the Word is spoken.[25] Like other monastic spiritualities, Carthusian spirituality is concerned with presence, God's presence. Guillerand stressed that we should all aim to remain focused as much as possible on that presence. Monastic solitude is a place for seeing God, face to face.

10. CISTERCIAN SOLITUDE: ALONE *TOGETHER*

When Abbot Robert of Molesme left the abbey in 1098 in company with Alberic, his prior, Stephen Harding, his sub-prior, and two other reform-minded monks, he had no idea of the historically significant monastic revolution his little band was setting in motion. They chose a lonely spot in the wilderness outside Dijon named Citeaux and built there what came to be known as the 'New Monastery'. Although Robert was forced to return to his abbatial responsibilities at Molesme after only a year at Citeaux, Alberic who succeeded him as abbot was able to hold things together during those most difficult early years and to establish Citeaux's spiritual formation. When Alberic died in 1109, Stephen Harding became abbot. His talent for administration, coupled with his erudition and experience, helped to fashion an order that possessed a clearly formulated programme with a firm legal underpinning. By the time of Stephen's death in 1134, seventy-five abbeys had already been founded in the still young Cisterican movement.

During the fourth year of Stephen's reign, Bernard (of Clairvaux) arrived on the scene with some thirty other companions in tow – family and friends. During this time Stephen developed the expansion of estates and grange systems for which Cistercians became so famous. There had already been need for a first foundation the year before Bernard's arrival, so Citeaux founded La Ferte. In the next two years they founded Pontigny, Clairvaux and Morimond, followed four years later by another five foundations. Citeaux led a monastic reform at a high point in the development of monastic life; it proclaimed a return to the letter of the *Benedictine Rule*, strict adherence in a radical movement of spiritual renewal. The Cistercian movement sought greater solitude, poverty and austerity. The twelfth century became the 'Cistercian' century, during which the new reform repopulated monastic Europe at an astounding rate.

Unlike the Carthusian and Camaldolese movements, the early Cistercian founders did not consciously model themselves upon the Egyptian desert forebears. The Cistercians of course knew the literary tradition –promoted by the *Benedictine Rule* – and desert imagery appeared in the works of second- and third-generation Cistercians, such as Bernard of Clairvaux and William of St-Thierry. But it had played little part in the lives and documents of the founders.[1] Although Cistercians were interested in the solitude offered by cloister in the wilderness, their foundations had to be located near enough to available markets for purposes of commerce. The Cistercians were Benedictine and definitely cenobitic, trying as much as possible to be self-sustaining and self-contained. What 'desert' they lived in was the spiritual desert of temptation and struggle.[2]

Separation from the world was a given. To live in monastic solitude one had to distance oneself from the turmoil of secular society and embrace the quiet and calm of the cloister. Even when the 'contempt for the world – *contemptus mundi*' theme rears its head in Cistercian spirituality (as it does in so many spiritual and monastic medieval texts), it does so more out of concern for the claustral quiet than for the noise beyond the walls. The Cistercian institution of *conversi* working in the fields and on the granges helped to allow choir monks to remain in the quiet of their cloister, separate from worldly concerns and distractions. Separation for the sake of listening and being present to God's Word is as valid today as it was in twelfth-century France. As for all monastics, the dialectic between separation from the world and openness to that world becomes a delicate balance between personal perspective and gospel demands. The monastic charism of hospitality always carries within itself a potential risk for disruption and disturbance. But the need for hospitality in today's world seems greater than ever. Each Cistercian and Cistercian community must find their way to being open to the world while remaining apart from that world.

Cistercians are part of the greater Benedictine tradition and as such, place a heavy emphasis on cenobitic life. In Benedictine monasticism, solitude came to the monk/nun by way of separation and silence within the cenobitic context – taken to its uttermost by the Cistercians. They were constantly together at work, in the church, refectory, fountain house, latrines and dormitory.[3] Never being alone made silence most expedient. For Cistercians whose exterior silence could be matched by interior tranquillity, solitude became a reality and, indeed, a necessity for contemplation. But the silence had to work. For communion to be possible, the wisdom of silence and solitude had to prepare the way.

BERNARD OF CLAIRVAUX

One can hardly imagine the excitement of the small community at the 'New Monastery' when Bernard, third son of Tescelin le Saur de Fontaines, and his thirty or so companions arrived to join the community. Certainly the most famous son of the twelfth century, Bernard was born in 1090, studied in Châtillon-sur-Seine and Saint-Vorles, and became a Cistercian at the age of twenty-one.[4] Bernard's entourage included his uncle Gaudry, his brothers, various relatives and friends. In 1115 Abbot Stephen sent Bernard to found Clairvaux where he was abbot until his death in 1153. During that time, he made 68 foundations, riding the crest of the incredible Cistercian wave throughout Europe. Not only was Bernard director of Citeaux's expansion, but also its doctrinal spokesman, writing at least nine major treatises, 332 authenticated sermons, and some 540 letters.

Bernard's personality shows through strongly in his writings, especially his sermons directed at his Cistercian brothers. He certainly must have been an extraordinary man who had equally extraordinary influence in motivating others to accomplish all that happened during the Cistercian century. Leclercq called Bernard's influence truly unique in monastic history.[5] He wrote passionately and often about renouncing and separating from the world. He pleaded with his monks to get the world out of their minds and hearts. The flip side of the vocational coin was to live the monastic observance with fervour and authenticity. Since the world can only offer what is temporary, Bernard wrote, it is best to renounce it. It is much better to leave the world and live a life of action and contemplation in the monastery, within the cloister. The cloister is a paradise, he wrote – echoing the words of Peter Damian and further back, the *Apophthegmata* – though here within a cenobitic context.[6] Bernard seemed very keen on the inner workings of community life, the various personalities within a community, and how human nature revealed itself in the cloister.

Though separate from the world, the Cistercian cloister was no escape from that world. The community had to deal with the world of politics in both Church and State, commerce, hospitality, etc. The abbot, prior, cellarer and porter – not to mention the many *conversi* working in the fields and on the granges – did not lack opportunities to meet reality outside the cloister. Bernard encouraged his monks to be united to all souls, to watch over all. He likened monks praying for the entire Church to teeth that chew on behalf of the whole body.[7] In Bernard's mind, the monk is not 'of the world', but definitely 'for the world'. Monks are to be contemplatives through prayerful solitude and silence.

The question of Cistercian solitude is tricky because it is difficult to imagine pre-twentieth-century Cistercians ever being alone. Bernard was very much the confirmed cenobite. He has nothing good to say about hermits or eremitism on the one hand, but is also significantly concerned that there should be a solitary dimension to his monks' life. Solitude in community is necessary to the monastic journey for Bernard, but outside community he has no time for it. His early Cistercian biographers wrote that it mattered not that Bernard had little time to be alone because he worked, read and prayed wherever he was. William of St-Thierry wrote that at Clairvaux every monk 'seemed' to be alone.[8] But 'seeming' to be by oneself and 'being' by oneself are two very different realities. For whatever reason(s), Bernard had nothing positive to say about hermits – at a time when eremitical movements were thriving in Italy, England and elsewhere. He echoes Benedict's cautionary words about the hermit life, without adding Benedict's positive statements about solitaries. He attacks those who have left their monasteries for the eremitical life only to become lukewarm, slack and dissolute.[9] One might cynically wonder if perhaps Abbot Bernard felt his plans for more foundations were threatened by would-be hermits in his flock? In any case, Bernard is soundly for solitude, as long as it is within a cenobitic context. Naturally, Cistercian silence became imperative, to allow an inner solitude to develop. Silence, however, was not an absolute, and allowance was made for necessary speech. Bernard's own favourite time for prayer was during the night silence when the other monks were sleeping.[10]

Monk and abbot, preacher and writer, founder and crusader, diplomat and doctor of the Church: Bernard of Clairvaux influenced many writers, schools and movements throughout the centuries, including the Cistercian school itself, Victorines, Franciscans, the great monastic women mystics of Helfta, the *devotio moderna*, etc. He was certainly gifted and probably, often enough, a 'difficult' personality. He was an eloquent spokesman for monastic solitude, if only within a strictly cenobitic ambit. His biographer, intimate friend and confrère, William of St-Thierry, proved far more positive regarding the various dimensions of monastic solitude.

WILLIAM OF ST-THIERRY

Born in Liège around 1085, William of St-Thierry (also known as William of Liège) was a noble who enjoyed the best educational opportunities of his day. As a monk of St Nicaise of

Rheims, he was elected abbot of the monastery of St-Thierry
in 1119. He had met Bernard during the preceding year and
over subsequent years was persuaded by Bernard to remain a
Benedictine abbot rather than transfer to the Cistercians. But
in 1135 William joined the young Cistercian foundation of
Signy in the Rheims diocese and remained a Cistercian monk
for the rest of his days. He made this transition in the name
of solitude.[11] During the 1140s William stayed at the charterhouse of Mont-Dieu, for which community he wrote his
celebrated *Golden Epistle*. He died in 1148 after spending
his final years gathering materials for the biography of his
intimate friend and mentor, Bernard of Clairvaux. William
was a prodigious writer whose literary output often came down
through the centuries attributed to the pens of other more
famous people (Bernard, for example). One is tempted to think
William was just as energetic and gifted as Bernard, but
simply lacked the name recognition during subsequent centuries. For our purposes, William's most important work is the
Golden Epistle.

As opposed to the first generation of Cistercians, William
was quite consciously aware of the desert witness of fourth-
century Egypt. He was not at all averse to claiming that desert
heritage and making it his own personal goal. Although he
claims Bernard was restoring the fervour of Egypt among his
brethren at Clairvaux,[12] this was more William's enthusiastic
interpolation than Bernard's conscious effort vis-à-vis Egypt.
William was keenly aware of the need for monastic separation
and was not at all averse to making the 'desert' connections
regarding solitude and silence. He developed a spirituality of
the monastic cell. William had his own personal cell as a
Benedictine abbot; when he became a Cistercian of Signy, he
was allowed a private cell by direction of the General Chapter
at Bernard's request. For William, the cell was the place of
encounter and union. The cell was sacred ground and a sanctuary,[13] where God dwells in the 'inward' cell of the conscience.

Solitude was a primary concern for William who considered
it consonant with being a monk. The cell was a battleground,

as it was for the desert tradition. Vices and bad habits follow
the monk into his cell and he must root them out of his heart,
so silence and solitude can flourish. Unlike Bernard, William
esteemed hermits; he championed the solitaries of Mont-Dieu
for bringing the desert to France.[14] Bernard had likened solitaries to animals wandering off from the herd; William
considered them fulfilled people in graced solitude.

William wrote of solitude, union and communion from personal experience. Consonant with the monastic tradition, he
considered union/communion the only goal of solitude, silence
and contemplative prayer. William of St-Thierry and other
luminaries of the second and third generations of Cistercian
spirituality helped ignite a taste for solitude, silence, contemplation and mysticism among generations of monastic seekers
of God.

THOMAS MERTON OF GETHSEMANI

The most eloquent spokesman and unquestionably the most
famous son of Citeaux in recent centuries was Fr Louis of
Gethsemani Abbey in Kentucky – Thomas Merton. His entire
monastic life seemed to be first a search for solitude, then a
struggle for the integrity of solitude (even eremitical solitude)
in the Cistercian life, and finally a deepening appreciation for
the solitude he lived during his last years. Merton was out-
spoken in his efforts to prove that hermits could, and should,
exist in cenobitic communities. Because he had such a talent
for touching the human heart in his writings about monastic
life and the spiritual journey, Merton enjoyed an immense
readership. He is as popular a spiritual writer today as he was
when he died in Bangkok, Thailand, in 1968.

As a young monk, Merton struggled with temptation to leave
the Trappists (reformed Cistercians) and join the Carthusians
for more solitude. Later on, he would revisit the temptation,
but this time thinking to join the Camaldolese. Of his own
volition, Merton did not join the Carthusians and later, under
obedience, he likewise did not join the Camaldolese. He

remained a Cistercian monk and fought on solitude's behalf his entire life, paving the way for countless monks and nuns, members of active orders, and lay solitaries to follow their vocations to solitude. This endeavour must have proved an overwhelmingly frustrating experience for him. The struggle only deepened over the years and finally resolved itself as Merton matured spiritually.

But Merton had to wait a few years from the time he originally asked his abbot for permission to live in a hermitage on the abbey property. He had developed a strong inner solitude at Gethsemani and now hoped to join it to a recognised physical solitude. Abbot James Fox evidently took seriously Merton's request and repeatedly 'dialogued' with him about solitude. Finally, Merton was allowed to become a hermit within the abbey's cenobitic community in 1965. These last three years of his life – 1965–68 – were the hermitage years. Some in his community criticised Merton for this move into a hermitage, but for him it was a matter of freedom, authenticity and inner necessity. Accused of being like Thoreau in the woods instead of like the Baptist in the desert, Merton countered that he just wanted to be himself, not really 'like' anyone else.[15]

For perspective, however, it is important to remember that Merton lived almost his entire monastic existence in a distinctly cenobitic context. The inner solitude promoted by Bernard of Clairvaux and William of St-Thierry was necessary to Merton's well-being. He described his own Cistercian tradition as a monastic movement that promoted a 'remote' approach to communal life with silence and isolation expected to provide solitude.[16] In point of fact, there have been Cistercian hermits over the centuries, though not many. The Cistercian Order was patron to numbers of hermits, anchorites and anchoresses. Some of their own numbers retired into solitary places.[17]

Thomas Merton became one of these solitaries. He saw solitude as necessary to the monastic quest. He considered separation and withdrawal from the world an important opening to solitude that needed to be respected. But Merton was not blind to the false solitude that is ego-centred and self-absorbed escape from community. True solitude is risky and perilous enough, for those who have already found God in community and been called into solitude.[18]

Merton saw a direct relation between true solitude and solidarity. One does not so much 'do' solitude as 'be' solitude; and one 'is' solitary to welcome the interrelatedness of beings in the compassion of love. Merton spoke for silence in a noisy world. The solitary has a vocation to silence; it is the air one breathes in solitude. Within this silence Thomas Merton was truly reborn. He spoke to us all in our hearts – that realm of silence. His message was universal, as universal as love. In Merton, contemplation bore an exquisite fruit, and the world is still feasting.

11. ANCHORETIC SOLITUDE: JULIAN OF NORWICH

Before we look at the distinctly anchoretic life as it developed in medieval England, it is probably timely to mention at this juncture all the countless hermits and wandering solitaries who inhabited Christendom during these centuries, outside the juridical framework offered either by membership in eremitical orders such as the Camaldolese, Carthusians and Grandmontines, or by attachment to some religious entity or institution. There were so many ways to live as a solitary. Within the institutional Church, the non-eremitical monastic orders made way, at times reluctantly, for hermits. Farmer[1] notes that traces of Benedictine hermits show up in every century until the nineteenth. Many more Benedictine women attached themselves as recluses to the male houses during the early medieval centuries when there were only a few Benedictine houses for women. And again, Cistercian communities were often quite helpful to hermits and recluses, funding their lifestyle or allowing it to happen on their property.

But beyond the contours of institutional religious, solitaries existed in abundance. Medieval England was filled with local hermits and recluses. Hermits also existed in Germany, but spontaneously here and there, not in any organised framework or movement. Western France became a stronghold for eremitical groups. Italy – home of Romualdians, Camaldolese, Avellaniti and Vallombrosans – seemed to be filled with eremitical fervour.

How did hermits outside the institutions survive? A solitary does not live on solitude alone. They subsisted by various means: alms and donations, gardening, bridge-building, ferrying, road-tending, road-repair, lighthouse-keeping, writing books, illuminating manuscripts and guarding shrines. They lived on islands, in marshlands, in deep forests, in caves and in towns (though most urban solitaries belonged to the Order of anchorites, at least in England). Some of these hermits became quite famous, namely, the literary ones who left written testimony to their solitary lives, such as the monk of Farne, Richard Rolle of Hampole, Simon Stock the hymnist, Thomas Scrope the historian, George Ripley the alchemist, Geoffrey the grammarian, and Symeon the compiler of meditation manuals.[2] Hermits, as a whole, enjoyed much more freedom of movement and expression than their very stable counterparts, the anchorites and anchoresses.

Anchorites were generally situated within an urban setting, often attached to a church building within an enclosed set of rooms. They were anchorites to pray and contemplate. People could be sure of their anchorite's whereabouts, for the anchorite was stationary by church approval and English law. Other titles were given to the anchorite: *inclusus* or *reclusus* (male), *inclusa* or *reclusa* (female), and *anachorita* (referring to either sex). A number of rules of life existed for the benefit of anchorites who were not members of orders. Those who canonically belonged to religious orders already had a rule. The ninth-century monk Grimlaic had written the *Rule for Solitaries* *c*.891. The Cistercian Aelred of Rievaulx wrote a rule for recluses for his own sister in the twelfth century. Both rules concentrated on external modes of behaviour, though not exclusively so. The *Ancrene Riwle* was a thirteenth-century guide for anchoresses. The *Dublin Rule* was written for male solitaries in the thirteenth century. Richard Rolle's *Form of Perfect Living* and Walter Hilton's *Scale of Perfection* dealt more generally with the solitary life. Both of these, along with the anonymous *Speculum inclusorum*, were fourteenth-century documents. All these rules (and still others) witness to the widespread popularity and presence of anchoretic spirituality over the centuries.

But there was something germane to the people, Church

and State of England that proved especially hospitable to the solitary life, at least until the sixteenth century. More than hospitable – in fact, the English seemed to be quite proud of their hermits, anchorites and anchoretic tradition. They supported them and protected them by law. Perhaps this was so because the Church itself in England tended to stand quite independent and self-contained. The life of individual solitariness must have appealed to their sense of 'English-ness', adventure and stark holiness. Often the anchorites formed bonds of support with their patrons, for whom they provided spiritual nourishment and intercessory prayers in their life of reclusion. Far from being perceived as anti-social misfits or marginalised, disturbed people, English anchorites were highly esteemed. Warren[3] states that people considered the anchorite's life the sanest lifestyle of them all. They located themselves at the very centre of the community, usually attached to churches, and did not isolate themselves from interaction with the people around them. As the worlds of politics, religion and culture whirled around them throughout the centuries, English anchorites continued on as a mainstay of community and ecclesial life, supported at all levels of society.[4]

Women who desired to live the solitary life in medieval England became anchoresses rather than female hermits. The latter category did exist, at least during the early medieval period, but the anchoretic life offered more security and protection of enclosure, with the physical support of patrons. Many English nunneries began as single cells for women solitaries. And in turn, some later women solitaries began their religious lives as members of established English nunneries. But in England anchorites and anchoresses belonged to the established 'Order of anchorites', whose life was considered even higher than the strictest monastic lifestyle.[5] They were considered, variously, penitents, intercessors, martyrs, ascetics and spiritual advisors. They were established as an 'order' by the law of the land and protected by law – giving another reason for women to become anchoresses rather than attempt the uncertain and unprotected life of the female hermit.

Most male anchorites tended to be priests and members of established religious houses before turning to a life of enclosure. Interestingly, the majority of women anchoresses were laity, though a certain number were nuns before entering the enclosed life. But the anchoretic Order ran the spectrum: single women, single men, married women, married men, widows and widowers, clerics, monks and nuns.[6] Anchorites were directly under the direction, sponsorship and juridical authority of the local bishop. The discernment of such a vocation fell to the bishop's discretion, and he questioned any prospective recluse before granting a license to perform the rite of enclosure. Often the bishop commissioned local abbots, priors, deans or canons to celebrate the actual liturgy of enclosure and receive the vows. This liturgy was intentionally reminiscent of the Mass for the Dead, and the recluse was sprinkled with dust in a symbolic act of burial into the anchorhold.

This anchorite's cell, or anchorhold (also called *reclusorium*), was the place for spiritual combat, harkening once again to that early monastic experience of the desert tradition. It was the place for contemplation and prayer, a penitential room, and one of martyrdom. This cell could consist of one or more rooms attached to a church building or chapel. A servant or servants, who lived with the anchorite, or nearby, used one window (sometimes, a door) to supply food. Another window opened onto the altar, so the anchorite could follow the celebration of Eucharist and receive communion. This window was sometimes referred to as a 'hagioscope' or the anchorite's 'squint'. A third curtained window could be used for chats with visitors, spiritual direction, confession, etc. – a window to the world, one might say. It was not always easy to find a vacant *reclusorium*, since they only became available upon the death of their inhabitants. Sometimes a cell was enlarged to accommodate a second anchorite, so that each had a separate cell with a communicating window.

One did not escape the permanent character of this enclosed lifestyle. Of course, that was the point of it. The vow was pronounced for life and wed one to the cell until death. During the early centuries of English anchoritism, the deceased anchorite was often buried right in the cell, so the solitaries knew that they were living in what would be their tombs. Sometimes the tombs were already fashioned before the enclosure, so the solitaries could always be mindful of death. The *Ancrene Riwle* actually encouraged the anchoress to dig up a bit of earth out of the future grave on a daily basis. Some anchorholds included small gardens or a courtyard for walking, but to leave the cell was forbidden, under pain of ecclesiastical excommunication. Even the civil law respected the anchoretic enclosure by allowing, in the case of litigation involving the solitary, a proxy to appear in his or her stead.[7]

But the anchorite or anchoress did not live in total isolation. They did have servants to attend to their physical needs, and these servants did sometimes live in the anchorhold with the solitaries. Sometimes those same servants became the successors to the solitaries they had faithfully served. Guests were allowed for various reasons, sometimes going into the very anchorhold itself, but rarely into the most solitary space. The *Ancrene Riwle* did allow for a cat in the anchorhold, probably for the practical reason of rodent control, but it only seems natural that the solitary would derive some companionship from a feline helper. Overall, life in the anchorhold was meant to be a rather austere affair. Most anchorites, if not all, surely dealt with temptations stemming from monastic *acedia* on occasion, and had to come to grips with boredom, apathy, laziness, perhaps even despair. But the various rules of life encouraged the anchorites to work hard to simplify their lives as much as possible. Though earlier solitaries tended to live primarily a penitential life, later ones steered away from extremes and were counselled to live moderately in the middle way. This seems eminently an English way to be – moderately austere.

What might an English anchorite or anchoress do, by way of service to the community? First, the purpose of contemplative solitude is contemplative prayer and a centring of the person

on God's presence and love. Tending towards union and communion by nature, contemplative solitaries served as powerful
centres of prayer and intercession at the heart of the town's
activities. Some anchorites were reputed to have been healers,
though their healing activity, on the whole, tended to be more
of a spiritual and/or psychological nature than the physical
healings that occasionally happened. They were soul-healers
and spirit-healers – consolers who would listen, empathise and
advise. Many were also sympathetic almsgivers who gave of
their surplus to less fortunate people. Individuals in the town
could donate funds to the anchorhold for that very purpose.
Some anchorholds became repositories for precious articles,
but generally this practice was considered a dangerous invitation to theft. For that reason, rules and advisory letters for
anchorites tended to dissuade solitaries from turning their
anchorholds into banks or treasuries.

There is some evidence that anchorites of a literary
character sometimes served as instructors to local children,
but anchoresses were discouraged (by the *Ancrene Riwle*, for
example) from becoming teachers for girls – though an anchoress's servant might well do so. An anchoress could embroider
or exercise similar skills whereby she could maintain a mind
fixed on the presence of God. Her male counterpart could be a
copyist for the same reason; many anchorites were
accomplished copyists. Later, in a time when anchorholds had
become centres of literary output, especially of a distinctly
mystical nature, solitaries could write to their heart's content.
During these later 'mystical' centuries (as opposed to the
earlier penitential ones), some anchorites became visionaries
and prophetic voices. But the anchoretic solitary always
remained a person of prayer for others. The anchorhold was a
place of compassion and empathy; by its stability, it became
a place of solitary solidarity with all. A prime example of
such solidarity was the fourteenth-century English anchoress,
Julian of Norwich.

JULIAN OF NORWICH

Thanks in great measure to the English Benedictine, Augustine Baker, and his school of spiritual thought, we know of the mystic Julian of Norwich and her visionary revelations. She lived in the fourteenth century, a period marked by upheaval and turmoil. The Black Death decimated the population of Europe, while disease plagued their cattle, and drought their fields. The Peasants' Revolt flared up against the gentry and nobility, including the landowning churches and monasteries. If that were not enough, one can add the Hundred Years' War, the Great Schism of the Church, and the Lollard controversy to the mix – producing an overwhelming sense of calamity and chaos in the general consciousness of the people.

Norwich did not escape the turmoil. Though not a coastal city of interest to marauding pirates, the city is on the Wensum River with access to the sea, and became a port of some significance. Norwich was a centre for the wool and cloth trade, so the noisy atmosphere of a mercantile hub would not have escaped the notice of an anchoress at St Julian's Church, a few hundred yards from the main road. The city's spot for execution was also near St Julian's, and many a Lollard met their end within earshot of the anchorhold there. Norwich was at that time second only to London, both in population and wealth, and also boasted of its great library in late medieval England.

We do not know much for certain about the anchoress Julian who authored the *Book of Showings* in fourteenth-century Norwich. She may have been a member of a religious community, perhaps the Benedictine priory of Carrow, just beyond the walls of Norwich. Carrow held the benefice of St Julian's Church at the time and would have had some voice regarding who might inhabit the anchorhold. Scholars conjecture from internal evidence in the *Showings* that Julian must have been born in late 1342, or 1343. Since the author of the preface to the shorter text of *Showings* states that Julian is still living in the anchorhold in 1413, we know that she lived to a ripe old age, by medieval English standards. A number of bequests from wills also attest to Julian's years in the Norwich anchor-hold. Margery Kempe mentioned in her own writings that she had visited Julian in her cell for spiritual direction *c*.1412.

We know that Julian's successor as anchoress of St Julian's in Conisford, suburb of Norwich, also took the name 'Julian'. Julian was not likely the given name of either, nor of any other anchoresses who might have lived as 'Julian' at Conisford. It was customary for an anchoress to adopt the name of the patron saint of the church or chapel to which she was attached. Our Julian did not write about her early life or the circum-stances surrounding her enclosure, other than what pertained immediately to the fact of her near-death experience and sub-sequent visions. We do not even know her real name or her educational background. She may have been educated as a nun; she may have found tutors in the Augustinian friary across from her anchorhold. But Colledge and Walsh insist that Julian was well trained in Latin, Scripture and the arts, as well as strongly influenced by patristic writers and some spiritual writers of the early medieval period, especially the Cistercian school.[8]

We also know that Julian of Norwich had a powerful religious experience, which she described in her *Showings*. During later life, she seems to have reached a comprehension of her experience. What we now have as the long text of *Show-ings* describes more fully the revelations she received. One of these insights that have received much attention in the twentieth-century revival of Julian's work is her reference to God as Mother. This was not an invention of Julian's; many similar references can be found in writers like Augustine, Anselm, Mechtild, and again, the Cistercian school of spiritu-ality. Julian is not so much concerned with sexuality (femininity or masculinity), but with the fullness of God (God as Mother/Father).[9]

Her theological synthesis and 'integration' is the whole point behind her revelations, enclosure as anchoress, and becoming a spiritual model. Julian seems to have it all together, altogether like that little hazelnut cupped by her hand in *Showings*. Many superlatives have recently been laid at Julian's threshold, but this 'unlettered' anchoress and mystic of God's motherhood can perhaps best be summed up in one word – balance. Her message does a wonderful job of balancing -isms and -ologies, and all our pairings of seeming oppositions into a simple and eloquent prayer of unity, oneness and communion. Above all, Julian of Norwich was there for us – and for all. Her life focused on the brokenness of the human condition. Her communion with God formed a life of prayer for all others.

12. THE RUSSIAN *STARETS*: SERAPHIM OF SAROV

The charismatic role of the fourth-century desert abba in Egypt found new ground on the steppes and in the forests of medieval Russia. Solitaries called *pustiniki* arose in northern wastelands and, as in Egyptian deserts, followers settled around solitaries. Before long, towns and settlements grew near what, in some cases, became huge monastic complexes. Occasionally, a charismatic figure would emerge from silence and solitude to function as spiritual director for others. Like the desert abba, this *geron* (in the Byzantine/Greek tradition) or *starets* (in the Russian tradition) was a discerner of spirits, exemplary teacher, and ascetic of the first order. The *starets* often functioned as confessor for his skete (community), as well as spiritual director for the young postulants and novices. His spiritual maturity was recognised by those around him who called him forth to the ministry of *startchestevo*. One did not plan or decide to be a *starets*. Although one could be recognised and designated a *starets* by an existing *starets* – clarifying the succession of ministry – others (like Seraphim of Sarov) followed no dynasty of *startsy*, but grew to spiritual maturity in silent, ascetical solitude, and found recognition.

Most of those who become *startsy* do so out of the ranks; they have usually not held hierarchical status or positions of power. Though the *starets* often functions as a confessor (when a priest), it is not the primary duty of a *starets* to do so. The *starets* is an advisor, healer, spiritual guide, 'seer' into souls, discerner of spirits, teacher, and courageous prophet of truth. By encouraging others to seek God in silence and solitude, the *starets* leads them to the very same spiritual path that prepared him or her for such work. The *starets* tries to help others to achieve a transparency of heart so they can discover who they really are. They move their disciples into paths of love and loving. It seems quite natural that this kind of spiritual ministry would open up the heart of *startsy* themselves beyond the confines of local time and place, history, politics and religion. Thomas Merton has indicated how the great figures of this spiritual movement achieved such a transformation that their evident compassion reached out to all humanity and creation.[1]

Kallistos Ware[2] has distinguished three gifts particular to the ministry of being a spiritual guide: insight and discernment; the ability to love and be compassionate; the power to transform the 'human environment'. The grace of discernment was considered absolutely necessary for living the Egyptian desert tradition. The depth of one's own self-knowledge and the perception of reality around oneself, combined with a creative intuition, allows the *starets* to pierce through the ordinary armour of human conversation to the core of another's inner depths. Trying to get to the very pith of life and love, the *starets* will sometimes sound illogical or irrelevant, perhaps even outrageous to the disciple seeking guidance. But the *starets* is concerned with the question the disciple should be asking. Someone as clairvoyant as Seraphim of Sarov reportedly was, could answer what was on a disciple's mind before words had even been exchanged, and then probe a far more complex and pithier area that had not even dawned on the disciple's consciousness.

The second of Bishop Kallistos' three gifts for a *starets* is the ability to love compassionately. That means the *starets* makes another's suffering his suffering. To be responsible for everything and everyone, as Dostoevsky's Starets Zosima would have it, the *starets* must become all heart – a heart transformed into the heart of Christ and transparent to the entire world. The third gift – the power to transform the 'human environment' – touches upon the miraculous in its ability to heal and transform reality, as it is normally perceived. The *starets* must be completely centred on God's presence at the centre of everything. Being at that centre can manifest itself in any number of ways consistent with the dynamics of the spiritual world that, at times, alter perceptions of 'reality' in the space–time continuum. And so, miraculous cures, telepathy, levitation, glowing bodies and trances abound in the literature about *startsy*. Should there be no *starets* available or recognised, spiritual seekers must make the common means of spirituality their *starets*: rule of life, *lectio divina*, penance, asceticism, prayer, etc.

One of the most famous *startsy* was St Sergius of Radonezh, the fourteenth-century Russian monastic founder and reformer. He is said to have had wild bears as friends, whom he fed with bread in his forest solitude. Disciples gathered around him, then others gathered around the resultant skete of monks. In time he and his disciples founded some forty monasteries before his death in 1392, by which time he was recognised as a *starets* throughout Russia. St Paissii Velich-kovsky (1722–94) was a Ukrainian monk on Mount Athos who drew so many followers that he transferred the group to Moldavia. His monks translated the many important patristic texts of the *Philokalia* into Slavic. Several of his followers became monks of Optina Pustyn monastery, where three other great *startsy* lived. Leonid (1798–1841) proved atypical of the *starets* mould, being quite fat, loud and vulgar, but a recog-nised *starets* all the same. Though Lev Danilovitch Nagolkine began his novitiate at Optina, he actually took the habit at Bélyé Béréga monastery where he became abbot and a recog-nised *starets*. There he met Starets Theodore, disciple of Paissii Velichkovsky. Once Leonid had renounced his abbacy, the two of them travelled to Valaam monastery and, later, to Optina, where he lived as *starets* for the remainder of his life. Although Leonid was huge, people saw him as tranquil, peaceful and joyous. He began a tradition of *starchestevo* at Optina, helped by Macarius who became his successor. But Leonid had enemies who used the local Bishop of Kalouga against him; he repressed and persecuted the *starets* until the latter's death in 1841.

His successor and good friend, Macarius (1788–1860) published many Christian mystical and patristic writings, and wrote many letters of direction that show his developed spirituality as well as his knack for common sense. Under Macarius, the fame of Optina's *startchestevo* spread universally throughout Russia, from peasants to the intellectual elite – touching upon the cultural, social and even political life of Russia, as well as its spirituality. Ambrose (1812–91) was designated successor to Macarius. Like all *startsy*, he had to deal with everything from theological debates and mystical visions to questions about marriage, politics and livestock. The silence and solitude that formed him into a *starets* became prized moments during his years of busy ministry. Dostoevsky is said to have probably based his characterisation of Starets Zosima on Starets Ambrose of Optina Pustyn, whom he knew personally. But perhaps the most famous *starets* of them all was Seraphim of Sarov.

SERAPHIM OF SAROV

Prokhor Moshnin was born in Kursk, Russia in 1759. He lived during the time of the French Revolution and the invasion of Russia by Napoleon's troops. His father died when Prokhor was only three. When ten, he experienced one of three major cures through the intercession of Mary, Mother of God. When eighteen, he made a pilgrimage to Kiev with a group of young men; while there, he visited Dositheus, superior of the monastic laura of caves at Pechersk, who told him to go to the Sarov monastery for his religious life. Two years later, he became a novice at Sarov in November 1778. At that time, permissions to profess religious vows in Russia were granted by the czarist government only reluctantly, so Prokhor's novitiate lasted eight years. He became a professed monk of Sarov on 13 August 1786, taking the name Seraphim. A year after his ordination to the priesthood, Seraphim became a hermit in the nearby forest, living as a 'stylite' on two large boulders for one thousand days. He was considered the 'St Francis' of Orthodoxy, communing with wild animals and at peace with all of nature. After six further years spent in a hermitage in the woods, recognised as a *starets* for his own community, as well as for nearby nuns and peasants, Seraphim was attacked and severely beaten by thieves who left him for dead. Seraphim managed to crawl back to Sarov where he recovered, though remaining crippled for the rest of his life.

After five months of recovery, Seraphim returned to his hermit life in the forest. In 1806 Seraphim refused the office of *higoumen* upon the death of the superior, at which time he entered a period of total silence, and ceased serving as *starets* for his own community (1807–10). He was forced to return to the Sarov monastery in 1810. The day after his return, following a meeting with the superior, Seraphim shut himself in his cell and continued his life of silent reclusion. Tradition holds that he daily made one thousand full body prostrations during this period. Finally he ended his reclusion in late 1813 and resumed an extraordinary ministry of *startchestevo* until his death in 1833.

Merton called Seraphim the greatest Russian mystic.[3] He has also been called the *starets* of light and contemplation. These are powerful accolades indeed, and the evidence seems to agree. Seraphim does seem a bit eccentric, but then all the *startsy* seem eccentric to some degree. Like his religious forebear, Sergius of Radonezh, Seraphim had his pet bear, but it seems that he added wolves and snakes to the menagerie of forest life he fed.

The person coming to see Seraphim underwent a little ritual – as was often the case with *startsy*. Seraphim had the visitor venerate an icon of Mary, Mother of God, or a crucifix, then drink a few swallows of holy water and eat a piece of blessed bread from the liturgy. There he stood, beaming: wearing a woollen cap, a white linen tunic, birch-bark peasant shoes and the large copper cross from his mother around his neck. What a gift it must have been to know him! Seraphim was quite ascetical even (perhaps especially) after being crippled by the attempt on his life. All his life he read the Scriptures, patristic writings and hagiography. He practised constant prayer, performed prostrations, wore iron crosses inside his tunic, and slept in a kneeling position. He liked to eat grasses and herbs. Truly this *starets* was like a fourth-century abba.

But Seraphim was not without his detractors and enemies. During the last third of his life, Seraphim discovered he had no friend in the superior of Sarov monastery – such a different experience from the nurturing support he had received from superiors during his earlier monastic career. Like Leonid of Optina, Seraphim incited jealousy and anger, as well as awe and reverence. His own community tried to erase his memory following his death.[4] Fortunately, the nuns of nearby Divéyevo, for whom Seraphim served as chaplain and *starets* for many years, kept documentation. When he died, Starets Seraphim was kneeling before his favourite icon of Mary, Mother of God. His cell was on fire from an overturned candle, though no one would likely have been surprised if Seraphim's inflamed heart had been blamed.

We do not have much in the way of Seraphim's writings. The most important source for his spiritual teachings – other than the oral tradition stemming from the Divéyevo nuns – is a conversation remembered and written down by Nicholas Motovilov in November 1831. He had been healed in the presence of Starets Seraphim just two months earlier, fifteen months before Seraphim's death. This record was later placed in an attic by Nicholas' widow after his death – only to be passed on by the same widow to a writer named Serge Nilus seventytwo years later. Nilus published the document in 1903, the same year of Seraphim's canonisation by the Orthodox Church.

Seraphim encouraged others to centre themselves on Christ, to focus on the light of Christ. He considered the ascetical life to be the 'active' life (vigils, fasting, prostrations, etc.), while the 'contemplative' life concerned the mind and heart turning towards God. He tried to emulate the monastic life of his favourite spiritual writer, Isaac of Nineveh, and spent a good part of his life reading the Scriptures, which he kept in a small bag attached to the sleeve of his tunic.

When his good friend and superior, Abbot Isaiah, died, Seraphim underwent his famous period of total silence. A man of perseverance who kept strictly to his self-imposed silence, Seraphim encouraged others to work at it mindfully, to maintain a fixed focus. He placed silence at the top of his ascetical ladder. He knew well the activities in a monastery, so he encouraged his monastic directees to grab and savour what solitude and silence they could. He did not romanticise solitude, but told young monks that the devil besieges a hermit.

Seraphim tried always to convince his fellow monks of the benefits of *startchestevo*, that heart-piercing, mind-reading spiritual direction employed by the *startsy*. This was especially true for the younger monks. What was important to Seraphim was to experience the power of the Holy Spirit. His life and witness lit up an entire generation of Russian Christians; and his message continues to inspire countless others with his glowing light.

PART FOUR: CONTEMPORARY PROPHETIC SOLITUDE: FROM THE ALONE TO THE UNIVERSAL

13. STARETS SILOUANE OF ATHOS: COMPASSION FOR ALL

Simeon Ivanovich Antonov was born in the village of Shovsk in Tambov province, Russia, in 1866. Of peasant stock, Simeon lived a life of hard work with his large family. With only a rudimentary education, he became a carpenter's apprentice and, at the insistence of his father, later performed his military service before becoming a monk. He was physically strong in his youth, loved to eat, drink and party. It is said that Simeon was known to drink as much as three litres of vodka without rolling under the table, and one Easter, he ate an omelette containing fifty eggs![1] He weathered two flirtations with danger: he almost killed a man in a village brawl; he had extramarital sex with a young woman from the village. At the end of his military service, Simeon and a companion travelled to see John of Kronstadt to seek his advice, prayers and blessing on Simeon's planned monastic venture. Not finding the saint there, Simeon left a message asking John's prayers that the world not keep Simeon from his monastic plans. From the next day onwards, Simeon envisioned the flames of hell around him, wherever he went. He soon found his way to the Holy Mountain, Mount Athos.

Simeon reached Athos in the fall of 1892, and entered the Russian monastery, St Panteleimon, where he confessed the sins of his past and began the life of a postulant. As a novice, Simeon experienced temptations to return to life in the world and marriage. His confessor helped him through his torment and difficulties. Praying before an icon of Theotokos, Silouane (his religious name) received the gift of unceasing prayer – something a monk may wait his entire life to receive. But he

also experienced severe trials and conflicts with demons, like
the Egyptian desert abbas. As a young monk he habitually
travelled to old Rossikon, an hour away from St Panteleimon,
where he sought out Starets Anatol for advice. Anatol, who
encouraged Silouane to keep his mind free of thoughts, felt
utterly amazed by the young monk.

Silouane intensely experienced the typical vacillations
between periods of graced presence and the hollowing 'abandonment' by God. His demons kept him on his toes, as he
practised his unceasing prayer and performed his asceticisms.
He experienced a vision of the risen Christ enlightening the
world with new life and beauty; Silouane realised he was
tasting eternal life. He later wrote that during his first year
in the monastery he had experienced the Holy Spirit. Fifteen
years later, when Silouane felt tormented by demons during
the night and prayed for help, he heard a voice telling him to
keep his mind in hell and not despair.[2] Starets Silouane would
spend most nights awake, in prayer, catching short periods of
sleep here and there. He much preferred the nocturnal solitude
and its opportunity for unceasing prayer to the possibilities
for sleep.

Silouane was named one of the stewards at his large,
flourishing monastery. He had some two hundred workers
under him in various workshops. He would make his rounds
and give instructions as needed, then spend some of his day
praying for all his workers, their distant families, and the
sufferings of all. The *starets* worked hard all his life, and
prayed even harder. His last few years were spent in perpetual
prayer. When his end drew near, Silouane moved to the
infirmary of St Panteleimon. He passed away serenely on 24
September 1938, as the community celebrated the Office of
Matins.

Though not an educated or learned man, Starets Silouane's
intense prayer life in monastic solitude fashioned him into a
wise and holy monk. Schooled in the gospels and patristic
writings, he became a teacher to others. He was a *starets* of
the heart. He was not one of those solitaries who feel the entire

world should be monastic, or that there is only one way to be a spiritual seeker of God. For Silouane, what mattered most was the ability to discern God's will and to conform oneself to that will. He loved monastic life, its rounds of choir, private prayer in solitude and the demands of community life. All the better, if God's will lead others to embrace that monastic manner of life on the Holy Mountain, or elsewhere. But God's will was consciously at the centre of Silouane's spirituality. In order to discern that will of God and to live by it, Silouane saw the virtue of humility as crucial and necessary. Archimandrite Sophrony noted that, when faced with all the complexities and potentialities of Christian culture – the learning, books, architecture, music, paintings, sculpture, poetry – Silouane ignored it all in order to live Christ's humility and love his enemies.[3]

Silouane's prayer was very personal, a matter of face-to-face talking with God. Because he experienced the gift of unceasing prayer for most of his life, the *starets'* prayer was an expression of his ongoing union with God. But the full power of that union manifested itself to Silouane when he faced the torments of hell and fought off despair in the experience of deeply felt humility. Silouane saw prayer (and much else) as a fruit of humility. But humility was Silouane's key to prayer that does not dissipate.

It was in the power of the Spirit that Silouane truly experienced the risen Christ. Through this same Spirit we are all enabled to know Christ, love Christ, and be moved to pray for one another and all others. And through the power of the Holy Spirit we learn to love gracefully. Loving engenders the Spirit and the Spirit engenders love. Starets Silouane knew intimately the ups and downs of the spiritual journey – knowing God's presence one moment and feeling abandoned the next moment – and his wisdom echoes the desert wisdom and traditional monastic wisdom: persevere, hang in there.

But what unique characteristic of Starets Silouane's life, personality and spirituality distinguished him during his own time, and afterwards? Surely there have been many holy solitaries on Mount Athos before, during and after the lifetime of Silouane the Athonite? What set him apart from all the others? It was his deeply felt message of universality. So many holy mystics and solitary saints throughout the centuries grew in love to a point where they could not help but cross over boundaries between people, religions and cultures, in order to proclaim the universality of God's compassion and humanity's response. And we love (or hate) them for their prophetic boldness, their daring to preach universal compassion. During the last quarter of the nineteenth and first quarter of the twentieth centuries, when the winds of ecumenical fervour and interreligious tolerance (let alone dialogue) blew only so slightly, Silouane insisted on universal love. One could certainly not have predicted such an outcome for a nineteenth-century illiterate Russian peasant who became a monk in a protected – even insular – theocratic enclave of monastic orthodoxy like Mount Athos! But there stood Silouane; and Archimandrite Sophrony tells us he was both loved and hated for it – even on Mount Athos. Silouane had his enemies who feared and despised his universal approach to spiritual life and gospel ethics.

At least two scholars have likened Silouane to St Thérèse of Lisieux in the Roman Catholic tradition. Olivier Clément[4] sees them both as lights in our darkness, standing in humility at the edge of hell and not giving in to despair. They both became renowned for their 'little' way, their wisdom, and their mission of universal love. Christian Portier[5] likens the two inner journeys at the level of grace where similarities between Silouane and Thérèse are astonishing. Both of them hold incredible appeal across religious boundaries because they dared to love everyone and lived their lives as vessels of communion for the entire universe, consciously so. Both reached out to a troubled, tumultuous world from a cell of solitude and touched that world with hearts bursting in the love of it all.

Why did Silouane make such a bold statement with his life? The answer lies in the simple complexity of Jesus Christ and his gospel of love. It is hard not to see Christ when reading

Silouane's simple words of compassion and gospel love. Silouane seemed to shed tears for humanity as Jesus wept for Jerusalem. His love reached out to humanity because Christ's love did so. In his lived silence and monastic solitude he was a living bond of communion with all of humanity. His gift of tears spilled out his love for the cosmos until it might coalesce around its God of compassionate love. He thought of his own existence as a singularly simple search for humble love.

Silouane desperately wanted all of creation to experience salvation, so he consciously took that intention into his unceasing, continuous life of prayer. He saw this intercession on behalf of all humanity – indeed, all creation – as his life's work in the power of the Holy Spirit. Starets Silouane shed tears and suffered because people were neither in union with God nor in communion with one another. The vision of the risen Christ that the young Silouane had witnessed during a liturgical service was a luminous Christ embracing the whole world – a vision Starets Silouane came to embody in his own life. He felt compassion for humanity trapped in various kinds of pride, and suffering the pains of hunger, conflict and hatred. He prayed for all humanity to receive God's love as he had experienced it. He felt this need intimately and prayed on a cosmic scale. And he urged all others to do likewise. He wanted everyone to know the new life he experienced and how he saw everyone – without any distinction – as his sisters and brothers.

The theme of 'loving one's enemies' became – along with humility – the central theme of Silouane's life and spirituality. He considered such love and prayer for 'enemies' as the only proof of true Christian spirituality and progress. He saw such love as the Taboric light, the fire appearing over the apostles, and the flame Christ came to give the earth.[6] Silouane saw universality as an absolute for monastic life. All monks are meant to be universal in outlook and in sensibility. The monk prays for the world; the monk exists for the world. Silouane's spiritual message was for everyone, as was his heart. His prayer knew no boundaries, nor does his popularity today.

He lived his solitude for the whole world, and the world is increasingly coming to recognise it.

14. CHARLES DE FOUCAULD: THE UNIVERSAL BROTHER

It would be difficult not to sound romantic when describing the life of Charles de Foucauld. Orphan, military cadet, soldier, playboy, explorer, monk, hermit, missionary, translator, priest and martyr: all of these designations describe facets of his life. He was born to an aristocratic family in Strasbourg, 15 September 1858. His parents died in 1864, orphaning him and his sister Marie (Mimi), two years his junior; their grandparents raised them. Charles attended military and cavalry schools. His substantial inheritance allowed him to live a dissipated life there and in Algeria where he was posted. He resigned from the army in 1882 and made detailed exploratory journeys in Morocco from then until 1884, publishing his findings as *Reconnaissance au Maroc* in 1888. In 1886 he met Abbé Henri Huvelin in Paris, who became Charles' spiritual director for the rest of his life. Though Charles wanted to enter a religious order almost immediately upon his conversion, Huvelin counselled a waiting period of three years, while asking Charles to visit various religious communities.

After becoming a Trappist monk at the Abbey of Notre Dame des Neiges as Br Marie Alberic in 1890, he moved to a poor Syrian foundation (Akbès) only six months later, at the invitation of his Trappist superiors. Even as a Trappist of a destitute foundation in a hostile environment, Charles struggled with the feeling that he was not doing enough until he could live as the poorest of the poor – and later, with the poorest of the poor. His superiors sent him to Rome for his theological studies, where, just days before his solemn vows, Charles convinced the Abbot General that he should leave the

Order and pursue his unique vocation. Charles moved to the Holy Land where he secured a position of servant/worker for a convent of Poor Clares in Nazareth. He refused the rooms offered him, opting instead to live in a small tool shed in the garden. During this period at Nazareth (1897–1900) he began signing his name as Br Charles of Jesus.

In 1900 he returned to France where he studied for the priesthood at his former Trappist abbey, with which he kept in correspondence throughout his life. The bishop of the Viviers diocese in which the abbey was situated ordained Charles priest in June 1901, as an 'unattached' priest of Viviers. He spent the remainder of his life in the Sahara desert where he lived near the Tuaregs, a nomadic tribe of Bedouin Muslims. He received permission to build his first hermitage at Béni-Abbès, a large oasis where hundreds of farmers and French troops lived. Charles stayed there until 1905, at which point he received consent from Moussa, the Tuareg leader, to build another hermitage at a more isolated plateau in the Hoggar area, Tamanrasset. He had hoped to found a community of hermits at Béni-Abbès, but could find no one who wanted to share his life in a formal way. Charles decided to live at Tamanrasset, serving the local Tuaregs in any way possible, and living a contemplative life in solitary adoration. He also studied the Tuareg language and transliterated their oral tradition into several volumes of works, published posthumously. In 1908 Charles received permission from Pope Pius X to celebrate a hermit mass without any attendants.

In 1909 Charles travelled four days south of Tamanrasset to a remote mountain where, at an altitude of 9,500 feet with spectacular views and no source of water, he decided to build yet another hermitage at Assekrem. The stone hermitage was finished in 1911, and Charles would occasionally stay there in solitude. Ali Merad, a Muslim writer, describes Assekrem as radiating with Charles' presence embedded in its silence and solitude.[1] A Christian hermit, Charles lived among Muslims in the Sahara. His was a unique calling – much too unique for some Tuareg nomads butting against French colonialism. On

1 December 1916 Charles answered the door of his fortified hermitage at Tamanrasset. Some thirty Islamic warriors seized him and bound him in a kneeling position. The fifteen-year-old boy guarding him with a rifle panicked and shot Charles in the head, killing him instantly. A tragic mistake perhaps, but within the context of anti-French and anti-Christian activities. Earlier, Charles had written about his daily intention of facing the day, expecting to be martyred by nightfall.[2] The hermit of Béni-Abbès, Tamanrasset and Asse-krem became a martyr of the Sahara in the early evening of December 1. He had spent his life trying to break down barriers and form a network of hearts.

Charles de Foucauld was quite literally a modern desert father. From his days of soldiering onward, he felt drawn to the desert. By the time he moved to the Sahara, he felt he could live in no other environment. He loved the desert, its silence and solitude.[3] But he had lived as a 'desert father' long before the Sahara experience. His life with the Poor Clares in Nazareth and in Jerusalem was solitary, ascetical and focused. He tried to live a starkly simple regimen of recollection. His was a nineteenth-century version of desert monastic spirituality's incessant prayer, stability and the holiness of the cell. There was plenty of *fuga mundi* (flight from the world) expressed by Charles in his letters and meditations as well, though he tempered his flight from the world by generously serving the desert nomads and farmers of his locality. They, in turn, respected Charles' holiness and selfless service. They called him a *marabout*, a holy man, an ascetic.

Charles of Jesus was primarily concerned about his monastic solitude. It was absolutely necessary for the kind of contemplative adoration he lived in both the Holy Land and the Sahara. Already, in Nazareth, he had lived a life of almost exclusive solitude. De Foucauld saw himself as living the hidden life of Jesus who had lived his first thirty years in Nazareth solitude – at least in Charles of Jesus' mind. He modelled his own prayer of adoration in Nazareth on Jesus' example.[4] Again and again he wrote of his 'hidden life' and Jesus. Solitude was a

refuge for Charles, where he could be far away from everything. He kept much of the night in vigil, praying to the Father
as Jesus had done on numerous occasions mentioned in the
gospels. He called this his practice of 'unfolding' his soul to
God. This beautiful image of 'unfolding the soul' is descriptive
of love and courting. Charles' prayers and meditations in solitude focused on being with the Beloved. This image of de
Foucauld in nocturnal solitude and prayer is quite likely an
apt description of much of the hermit's adult life. He described
the Nazareth portion of that life in just such terms.[5]

But Charles de Foucauld's focus widened a bit when he
pursued priestly ordination and moved into the Sahara desert.
He did not lose the eremitical thrust to his spirituality; if
anything, his hermit vocation grew more pronounced and
refined. And part of that refinement was Charles' growing
concern about the universal salvation of the world. Already in
his younger years, Charles wanted to help break down barriers
between peoples and religions, hoping to construct a universal
brotherhood.[6] He prayed for universal salvation and, later on,
worked for universal understanding as he came to believe
more in universal salvation.[7] People came to recognise Charles
of Jesus as an ecumenical figure, a monk of universal appeal,
a *marabout* of interreligious significance. His simple lifestyle
as a Christian hermit in a startlingly new non-Christian
environment spoke eloquently to his fellow Christians and
deeply to his local Muslim sisters and brothers whom he served
in so many ways – feeding, doctoring, counselling, arbitrating,
teaching, praying. Ali Merad wrote a beautiful testimonial to
the person and power of Charles de Foucauld, a spiritual
master whose message sings out to all generations of oneness
and eternity.[8]

Not only did Charles of Jesus appeal to the Tuareg Muslims
in his vicinity through his generous lifestyle, but he also intentionally wanted to open up that appeal on a universal scale.
He wanted to be known as the 'Universal Brother'.[9] He knew
that, like charity, universal fraternity begins at home. Charles
of Jesus tried not only to be a brother to all, but also their

servant, especially among those whom he saw as the poorest and most needy, the abandoned and socially marginalised people with whom he shared an austere desert existence. Charles saw himself as a little brother of Christ and a brother to all, but especially to the poor and abandoned for whom there were no priests. Of necessity, but certainly by desire, he became an apostle of the poor for the sake of Christ. It sounds odd that a hermit contemplative would feel so driven to be actively involved in Tuareg medical care, social work, arbitration and politics. This seeming dichotomy puzzled the hermit as well, though he knew he must live out his vocation in that fashion.

In 1896 de Foucauld had written a small rule for a congregation he hoped to found in the Holy Land – the Little Brothers of the Sacred Heart of Jesus. By 1898 he was formulating a rule for a future congregation to be called Hermits of the Sacred Heart. In early 1899 he added his insistence on the priesthood and apostolic work to the rule. In 1902 he wrote an almost identical document for the future Little Sisters of the Sacred Heart of Jesus. But during the final years of his life, Charles of Jesus strove to organise a lay body – the Union of Brothers and Sisters of the Sacred Heart of Jesus. At his death, forty-nine people belonged to this group. Today several religious congregations for men and women, groups of priests, pious unions, sodalities and fraternities look to Charles de Foucauld as their patron and form their lives on his spiritual principles of poverty, hospitality and contemplative adoration. The unique vocation of de Foucauld's monastic solitude combined with focused apostolic work among the world's most destitute – and in a non-Christian environment, at that – left an amazing legacy of universal outlook in contemplative adoration and a startling embrace of poverty and simplicity centred on the poorest, the destitute and those abandoned by society.

15. JULES MONCHANIN: PASSION FOR THE UNIVERSAL

On 10 April 1895, at Fleurie en Beaujolais near Lyons, France, Jules Monchanin was born. He was a sickly child, and endured ill-health throughout his life. Drawn to books, he became one of the shining intellectual lights in France between the two world wars. Ordained a diocesan priest in 1922, Monchanin then obtained a licentiate degree in theology, before disappointing his professors and fellow scholars who were encouraging him towards the stellar academic career they had envisioned for him, by precipitously dropping any plans for a doctoral programme. Instead, he spent three years in parochial ministry, followed by time spent in orphanage care and a boys' boarding school, when health problems prevented him from further parochial work. On 26 March 1932, Jules Monchanin suffered a near-death experience, at which time he promised God he would devote his life to India, if he were to recover.[1]

From that time onwards, Monchanin pursued his quest for India. He first spent a period of study at a Jesuit training school in Belgium, during which time he spent a year studying Tamil and English. In 1938 he entered the Société des Auxiliaires des Missions. Monchanin had to worry about obtaining permissions for his Indian venture from both ends – France and India. Finally, in May 1939, he was able to take a ship out of Marseilles for his beloved India. Already in Belgium, he had a vision for his life in India: creating a contemplative Christian monastery for men and women.[2] Monchanin was highly respected among intellectual circles in France. People like Henri de Lubac and Louis Massignon were lifelong friends and supporters of the diocesan priest, following his star to the

East. Since he was always a bit of a maverick, standing on the margins rather than the centre line, Monchanin's move to India was perhaps secretly applauded by some in ecclesiastical circles.

Fr Jules' first ten years in his adopted country were a painful, difficult time. His letters from this period reflect his language struggles, bouts of loneliness and complications arising from his lifelong asthmatic condition. He was most fortunate to have found a welcoming, supportive bishop in Bishop Mendonça of Tiruchirappalli. Monchanin spent these early years studying the language and caring for parishes that needed pastoral replacements. In 1950, the Benedictine Henri le Saux joined Monchanin in India, and together they founded a monastic ashram on the Kavary River. Although these two men had very different personalities and ideas for Saccidananda Ashram, they managed to stay together, publish their ideas for Indian Christian monasticism, and plant their roots for this monastic presence in the future. By the time Monchanin and le Saux parted ways, the former was ailing and had to return to France for medical treatment. Monchanin's health deteriorated, and he was unable to return to India before death. After receiving Eucharist on 10 October 1957, Jules Monchanin stretched out his arms in the form of a cross and quietly died a few hours later.[3]

Monchanin's profound wish to die on Indian soil was denied him. He had written that he wanted to be buried in the earth of India, like de Foucauld in the desert sands of the Sahara.[4] Bede Griffiths, the English Benedictine monk who took over the ashram from its two founders, would bring it into the Camaldolese Congregation of the Benedictines, and build up the native Indian membership of the community. Griffiths added to Monchanin's own reflection about his similarities with Charles de Foucauld, writing that, like de Foucauld, Monchanin did not live to see a community build up around him, but died while planting the roots of the contemplative life in Christian India, just as de Foucauld planted those roots in Muslim Africa.[5] Jules Monchanin was a diocesan priest, but a most monastic one. He had a mystical temperament that reached out and embraced spiritual traditions of wisdom. He did so prophetically and courageously. His biographer, Françoise Jacquin, writes that he remained an extremist to the end, bonding with both the despised outcasts of India and the intellectual upper classes.[6]

Monchanin had been in India during the years of World War II, years that proved isolating and somewhat distressing for him. He felt frustrated by the lack of interest in Hinduism around him, among Christian missionaries and intellectuals, as well as among the native Indian Christian clergy. He did find some kindred spirits among intellectuals in India whom he met at various libraries where he researched or at conferences he attended where he often delivered erudite and challenging addresses. He formed lasting friendships with a Tamil priest named Arokiam, and with Pierre Ceyrac SJ. They were people to whom he could confide his dream of founding his group of contemplatives.[7] He found himself periodically discouraged, but never despondent. Over time, the desire to live an Indian form of solitary life took strong root, until a sojourn spent at the Jesuit novitiate at Shenbaganur confirmed him in that goal. He felt grasped by desire for silence, solitude and the anchoritic life.[8]

Jules Monchanin believed in his vocation to India. He longed to be silent in the silence of India. He and le Saux were both later to write about the possibilities of Indian Christian solitaries living near the great Indian pilgrimage centres and in poor villages, as well as in the isolated mountain and forest spots near the banks of holy rivers.[9] Simply to be in India was important, but to do so in an Indian manner was more important. Before le Saux joined him in India, Monchanin could only live his solitude because he was unable to gather others into the contemplative group he wanted.

Finally, in 1950, with the collaboration of le Saux and the co-operation of the bishop of Trichy, Monchanin formed an ashram dedicated to Saccidananda on the Kavary River. Both took Hindu names: Monchanin became Swami Paramārubyānandam; le

Saux became Swami Abhishiktananda. They celebrated their dedication ceremony with the bishop and a few sympathetic Indian clergy on 21 March 1950 – the feast of the *transitus* (passing) of St Benedict. Then they began their ashram life together. They felt the ashram (today known as Shantivanam Ashram) must be totally Indian, totally Christian and totally Benedictine. They wore the Indian *kavi* as a habit, enjoyed a simple vegetarian diet, read the Vedas and Bible for *lectio divina*, and slept on straw mats. They felt they were returning to a simpler, more primitive monasticism. They wanted to combine Subiaco with the 'laura' life of Palestine and the Egyptian desert tradition, so that Indian vocations could come forth and discover themselves in a contemplative monastic setting.[10]

Monchanin and le Saux wanted to be Indian Christian monks, but in the Hindu way. Their ashram was a definite departure from traditional Christian monasticism in the West. They wanted their life as simple and as poor as that of their neighbours. They wanted to be free. Monchanin sought to simplify the flow of life as much as possible, so that Hindu wisdom and Christian truth might be wed. At that crossroads, he chanted, meditated and prayed for the universe. The monastic quest, whether dressed in a black habit, a white cowl or an orange *kavi*, remains the same: to live mindfully and vigilantly in the presence of the sacred.[11]

Solitude was important to Jules Monchanin throughout his life. Already during childhood he had grown accustomed to being alone. For considerations of health he studied in a tutorial arrangement at home. Cerebral by nature, Monchanin spent much of his childhood years in solitary thought and private meditation. He would later write about a favourite tree in which, as a child, he would relish the silence he found there. He felt that he had learned to think and meditate then, in that tree.[12] Monchanin came to feel the necessity for solitude in his life, as well as the ever-deeper yearning for silence.[13] For him, the monastic is called away to be separate in order to live 'alone with the Alone'.[14] Monchanin thrived in silence and was known as a man of silence. He was eloquent about silence, considering it indispensable, 'festive', to be savoured, pure adoration, and open surrender to God.[15]

Jules Monchanin did sink himself into a life of contemplative adoration and prayerful intercession for the universe. The writings of Pierre Teilhard de Chardin had deeply affected Monchanin's own spirituality. Thus his prayer life reached out cosmically – forward in space and backward in time. Universality became his *modus vivendi* in Christian spirituality. Monchanin and de Foucauld truly were kindred hearts in that great spiritual network of hearts that keeps the perspective of humanity attuned to the 'Within' (Monchanin) and the 'Beyond' (de Foucauld). When writing to de Foucauld's disciple Louis Massignon, Monchanin referred to the vocation to universality they shared.[16] Françoise Jacquin[17] defined Monchanin's spiritual quest in a nutshell as a vocation for universality.[18] For Jules Monchanin, the only Church was the Church Universal – ever new and open to all. This was the Church for which Monchanin worked tirelessly and about which he wrote so passionately. Jules Monchanin had a special love for India, but a vibrant passion for the entire cosmos, the universe pulsating with the life and love of God.

16. CATHERINE DE HUECK DOHERTY: THE LITTLE MANDATE

Catherine Kolyschkine was born in 1896 in a railway car at Novgorod, where her parents had travelled to attend the great fair. She was baptised that same day in a Russian Orthodox church because Novgorod did not have a Roman Catholic church. She would later marry in the Orthodox Church and throughout her life, Catherine hoped and prayed for the reunion of the two churches. As a child she was attracted to church buildings and would spend time sitting in the quiet darkness of a church. She also recalled in her book *Poustinia* how she would accompany her mother on regular visits to a local *poustinik* (*starets*) when her mother sought spiritual direction.

Catherine's family moved a fair amount during her childhood. From Russia they moved to Turkey for a year, then to Greece for a while, before moving to Egypt for many years. Another year in France preceded the family's return to Russia. Catherine married her first cousin, Baron Boris de Hueck, in 1915. Since Riga was the family's ancestral city, the young couple began life together there, where Boris continued his architectural studies, although he was equally accomplished in engineering, astronomy and art. With the onslaught of war, Boris joined the Russian Army's Engineering Corps while Catherine became a battlefield nurse. During the subsequent Communist Revolution, the couple moved to Finland after some months in revolutionary Petrograd. At the family's Finnish estate, they eked out an existence surrounded by pockets of communists. Rescued by government forces, they moved to Murmansk. Working there with an international group mobilised against communism, Catherine eventually secured their passage to Great Britain where she worked at a hospital in Edinburgh. After some time in London, Catherine and Boris were allowed to immigrate to Canada. Catherine spent the entire trip on a stretcher; she was pregnant with her son George. They settled in Toronto for George's birth.

Having suffered incredible obstacles to their marriage's success and happiness, Catherine and Boris each ended up going their own way. Boris moved to Montreal where he had found employment and Catherine moved to New York City, after placing George with a neighbour of the Toronto parish whose pastor was encouraging her to find work in New York. Life there was a constant struggle for her (she now called herself Katie Hook) and she came very near to suicide. She found herself on the Brooklyn Bridge one night, but saw Christ's reflection in the water and ran back to the city.[1] Fortunately she made a chance connection with a Miss LaDelle who offered Catherine a job speaking on the Chautauqua circuit in the United States and Canada. Catherine became a very successful lecturer. She later quit the circuit due to harassment and threats by Soviet diplomats.

One day Catherine upended her purse, scattering bits and pieces of paper inscribed with Scripture quotes and recollections of a recurring dream. Forming these fragments into some order, Catherine found what she began calling her 'little mandate'. This mandate led her to sell her possessions in order to be poor with the poor, live simply, preach the gospel without any compromise, pray always and spread love.[2] She took this mandate to Archbishop Neil McNeil of Toronto, who supported her in her vocation, but asked her to wait out one year of discernment before acting on it. Finally, she received McNeil's blessing for her ministry to the poor in Toronto. Her Friendship House – staffed by herself and the young men and women who joined her in her endeavours on behalf of the poor – took care of the poor in her immigrant district of Toronto. McNeil handed Catherine a copy of *The Catholic Worker*, suggesting she meet with Dorothy Day, the woman responsible for its publication, and even paying her fare to New York City. Catherine had originally envisioned a solitary *poustinik* vocation for herself, out of which she might help the poor, but her work with Friendship House drove her into the fray. Some of the people who were drawn to witness the remarkable events at Friendship House were: Fr Paul Furfey, Dorothy Day, Peter Maurin, Fr Virgil Michel OSB, Fr Godfrey Diekmann OSB, Fr Gales, Jacques Maritain and Étienne Gilson. But this notoriety did not bring Catherine de Hueck happiness because she wanted to live her *poustinik* vocation rather than an active lay apostolate. She had originally envisioned herself alone, living the hidden life with occasional humble work among the poor.[3]

Catherine was amazed to find Dorothy Day involved in much the same activities of lay apostolate in New York City as she was at Friendship House in Toronto – feeding and caring for the poor by praying and begging. Catherine became, more or less, Dorothy's Canadian contact for *The Catholic Worker*. Her Toronto staff and volunteers sold the paper in the Catholic churches throughout Toronto. Through Dorothy, Catherine came to know many more important and influential Catholics, some of whom were to help in her endeavours with the Canadian poor. Unfortunately, people and events conspired to bring down Friendship House in Toronto by accusing Catherine of parental neglect, treason and communist affiliations. She left Toronto for New York City, where Dorothy Day met her at the train station and took her to the Catholic Worker. The Russian immigrant whom Fr Paul Furfey called 'Canada's Dorothy Day' was back in New York City, but not for long.

Fr Theophane Maguire of *Sign* magazine offered Catherine a job as a travelling author for *Sign*, writing a series of articles about Catholic Action in Europe. In Portugal she visited Premier Salazar, various workers, and Fatima. She found herself caught up in the Spanish Civil War, where she travelled to investigate the Falangists. She witnessed horrible atrocities and was treated shamefully. In France, Catherine acquainted herself with the Young Christian Workers, Young Christian Students, various adult forms of Catholic Action, co-operatives, credit unions, labour movements, the 'Little Brothers of the Poor', the Companions of St Francis, the Cerf publishers, and La Pierre Qui Vire retreat centre. In Belgium she observed the Young Catholic Workers, Independent Youth, the Young Farmers and Belgian labour unions. In 1939 *Sign* sent Catherine to Poland to see how Catholics were faring under Nazi occupation. She witnessed mass migrations of refugees from the Polish holocaust that she herself escaped by fleeing to the Hungarian border. This assignment had reminded her too much of her wartime frontline activities in Russia, and she returned to the United States.

Back in New York City (Harlem), Catherine opened another front of her own in the war against poverty by speaking out on behalf of racial justice. The whole question of race in 1940s America was quite volatile, as Catherine soon discovered. She encountered rejection, disdain, outright hatred, and death threats from Christian (including Catholic Christian) whites. Even Catholic universities of the Northeast tried to squelch her fervour on behalf of racial justice and interracial relations. During this Harlem sojourn, Catherine de Hueck met Eddie Doherty of *Liberty* magazine. By the time she had relocated to a Friendship House in Chicago, the two of them were in love. Bishop Sheil in Chicago married them on 25 June 1943. Catherine continued her work with Friendship House in Chicago until 1946, when she felt rejected by the staff.[4] She and Eddie moved back to Canada in 1947, where they fixed up an old house near Combermere, Ontario. This was the beginning of Madonna House, where those who came under Catherine's influence developed a lay apostolate, living by her 'little mandate' and initiating a *poustinia* movement in North America. She had taken her 'little mandate' into Friendship House and then to Madonna House where, by the 1970s, the group was taking vows of poverty, chastity and obedience.[5] Eddie Doherty died in May 1975, after living the last years of his life as an ordained Eastern rite priest at Madonna House. Catherine lived on for another ten years, involved in the growth of Madonna House ministries, and able finally to enjoy increasingly more *poustinia* time. She died at the age of eighty-nine in December 1985.

Catherine de Hueck Doherty had always felt drawn to solitude. During her long life, much of solitude's call was answered in bits and snatches of quiet aloneness in the midst of her lay apostolic work. Only in her later years did she allow herself to spend long periods of *poustinia* away from ministerial demands. She had an immense capacity for love and knew that love was necessary to healthy solitude.[6] She knew from experience the gift of loving God in the freedom of solitude's embrace.[7] To maintain that solitary experience in the marketplace, Catherine encouraged a mindfulness consonant with her Eastern roots – using the 'Jesus Prayer' to centre on God's presence.[8]

Much of what Catherine wrote about solitude applied equally to the practice of silence. She connected silence with communication, peace, love, wholeness and mystery.[9] Bringing silence and solitude together into an experience of *poustinia*, Catherine was able to promote in the West spirituality from the East. She saw her entire life as a vocation to *poustinia*, in solitude and silence.[10] The entry into the inner desert allowed her to 'be' and pray for others in a concentrated fashion. Her Madonna House movement promoted *poustinia* for the benefit of the Church.[11] Sounding like a desert amma, Catherine wrote that the *poustinik* fashions the desert into a garden.[12] But the garden was meant to be seen by all. Catherine felt as though she were God's bird sent out to tell the good news to the entire universe.[13] In her wisdom she echoed the ecclesiology of the eleventh-century hermit Peter Damian's *The Lord Be with You* by accenting how the entire Christian community was present to her, and in her.[14] Catherine deeply felt the efficacy of prayer in her *poustinia* movement – in terms of cosmic dimensions.[15] Her ministry strove to open up contemplation's door to everyone, suggesting *poustinia* to all, and offering *poustinia* for all who might come to Madonna House.

Catherine helped to make monastic solitude and silence accessible to everyone, and tried to make contemplation part of everyone's vocabulary. By the end of her life, she considered her entire existence an exercise in *poustinia*, with her service and ministry being echoes of its solitude and silence.[16]

17. DOROTHY DAY: SOLIDARITY WITH THE POOR

Born in Brooklyn on 8 November 1897, Dorothy Day was the middle child of five and grew up in New York, Oakland, California and Chicago. The family's brief sojourn in Oakland where Dorothy's father was a sports writer in the Bay Area, came to a sudden end in 1906 with the catastrophic earthquake that devastated San Francisco. Dorothy carried the memory of that fateful night's awakening throughout her life. After the family moved to one of the poorer sections of Chicago, she came face to face with some of the numbing sadness of poverty. Though the Day family was Episcopalian, Dorothy quickly chose the workers' battle against poverty and unjust conditions as her 'religion' when she became a freshman at the University of Illinois – Urbana, where she joined the Socialist Party. Dorothy found the meetings rather boring in Illinois and jumped at the chance to adopt a more activist stance in New York City after only two years of undergraduate studies. She moved to New York with her family and became a reporter for a socialist daily newspaper, *The Call*, and an IWW (International Workers of the World) card-carrying member.

She followed this job with a series of others related to unionising, pacifism, social reform and anarchy. Dorothy worked as a freelance writer from 1917 to 1927, during which time she spent her first jail confinement at Occoquan Prison, when she and her fellow advocates of women's suffrage were arrested and later placed in solitary confinement to punish their hunger strike. Dorothy's life was that of an activist who always found acceptance among anarchists. As a woman in her late seventies, she would write that she was accepted by anarchists as one of their own because she had been arrested eleven times, never voted and never paid federal income taxes.[1] For a while, she was a fairly constant companion of Eugene O'Neill in the Village and was known to have followed up long nights of drinking with him by slipping into a rear pew of St Joseph's where she found some comfort and quiet.[2]

She became a nurse trainee at King's County Hospital in Brooklyn, where she fell in love and became pregnant. She chose to have an abortion in a futile attempt to hold on to her lover – an action she regretted her entire life. In 1924, she published an autobiographical novel (*The Eleventh Virgin*) about this abortion episode and used the five thousand dollars she made by selling the filming rights to purchase a cottage on Staten Island. There she lived a common-law marriage with another anarchist, Forster Batterham, an English-born biologist. In the happiness of those days, Dorothy picked up the Bible – as she had done in Occaquan Prison under less happy circumstances – and felt herself drawn to prayer. She became pregnant again and gratefully gave birth to her daughter, Tamar, in March 1926. Through the assistance of a Catholic nun whom she met on the Staten Island beach, Dorothy had Tamar baptised a Catholic – something she personally wanted to experience. Knowing that Forster would have nothing to do with her if she became Catholic, Dorothy spent an agonising year marked by bitter verbal battles with Forster whom she deeply loved, before choosing the Catholic Church and a life without Forster. Dorothy Day would experience this period as her first conversion. She would see Staten Island, the sea, and the world of nature opened up for her by Forster as contributors to her conversion, but her times of solitude gave her the glimpses of God she had to follow.

A second conversional moment occurred in 1932 when she attended the Hunger March of the Unemployed in Washington DC and watched the demonstration of the poor empowered by their political action. Dorothy walked to the National Catholic Shrine of the Immaculate Conception to pray. It was actually the feast of the Immaculate Conception. She wept and prayed that God might give her direction how to use her talents on behalf of the poor and workers of the world.[3] When she returned to New York City, Dorothy found Peter Maurin waiting at her apartment. A French personalist and former Christian Brother who had a high regard for Benedictinism, Maurin had a community plan: living in harmony, sharing the fruits that manual and intellectual labour had brought civilisation, respecting silence, and worshipping communally.[4] The Catholic Worker movement was born. *The Catholic Worker* newspaper, houses of hospitality for the poor, and later, farm communes, became Catholic Worker hallmarks.

Daily life in the hospitality houses included prayer, reading, spiritual instruction and seminars, work, and all the dynamics of communal life. Then, as now, Catholic Worker life was demanding. The movement championed the poor, opposed nationalism and war, supported workers' rights and agrarian reform. Dorothy gave herself tirelessly to the movement throughout her life. She succinctly described her average Catholic Worker day as beginning with early morning mass and the Divine Office, and ending at midnight.[5] The movement grew rapidly and hospitality houses sprang up around the United States, but suffered severe setbacks prior to World War II, when the Catholic Worker established a neutral stance of non-violent pacifism. During the fifties, many Catholic Worker members became peace activists who endured long prison sentences. Dorothy herself was no stranger to jails. Even at the age of seventy-five, she was arrested while picketing with the United Farm Workers.

Despite Dorothy's feisty nature and sometimes controversial stands, love always remained her primary focus. She considered love the foundation of the Catholic Worker movement. And that love took Dorothy Day on many travels on behalf of the poor, workers, peace, and the movement itself. She travelled to Europe, Asia, Africa, Canada, Mexico and Cuba. By the time she died at the age of eighty-three on 29 November 1980 Dorothy had prophetically changed the face of American Catholicism in relation to peace, poverty, work and prayer.

Those last two words – work and prayer – bring to mind
Dorothy's connection with monastic solitude. She had an early
knowledge of the desert abbas. When she eventually decided
to become a Benedictine oblate, Dorothy wrote that she felt
Helen Waddell's *The Desert Fathers* was the book most responsible for her oblation.[6] Though she never lived in a desert,
Dorothy savoured desert spirituality. When she came into
contact with Peter Maurin in 1932, she became acquainted
with the Benedictine tradition so dear to Peter because the
Benedictine Rule was written for rural communities of layper-
sons. Dorothy would later write in her *Catholic Worker* column
that she claimed St Benedict as her patron because 'Work and
Pray' was his motto.[7] Peter Maurin based much of his reform
plan on Benedictinism, and Dorothy, who considered Maurin
her lifelong mentor, looked to Benedictines for guidance. Her
love of Scripture and the practice of *lectio divina* placed her
in good monastic company.

The monks of St John's Abbey in Collegeville, Minnesota
were early financial supporters of the Catholic Worker movement. Dorothy became a good friend of Virgil Michel, a monk of
that community and leader of the twentieth-century Catholic
liturgical reform movement. Michel was key to the founding
of the Liturgical Press, as well as the journal *Orate Fratres*
(later *Worship*). Her friendship with Michel and subsequent
familiarity with the liturgical movement helped Dorothy to
form her opinions about community living. Hospitality is a
hallmark of Benedictine tradition – something intimately
important to Dorothy and the Catholic Worker movement.
Much of Dorothy's efforts were devoted to their houses of hospitality, farm communes and rural retreat centres. Jim Forest
would write that Dorothy gave witness to hospitality as a way
of life.[8]

Another important Benedictine for Dorothy was Rembert
Sorg, a monk of St Procopius Abbey in Lisle, Illinois, who wrote
Towards a Benedictine Theology of Manual Labor. Dorothy
wrote about this book in the October 1949 issue of the *The
Catholic Worker*, culling insights for her own spirituality and

the further development of the Catholic Worker movement. Another of Dorothy's collaborators at the Catholic Worker, Stanley Vishnewski, claimed that without its Benedictine influences – hospitality, guesthouses, farming communes – there would have been little to the Catholic Worker programme.[9] Like St Benedict who called his monastery a 'school of the Lord's service', Dorothy called the Catholic Worker a school[10] where some might spend a short period, others a lifetime.

Dorothy had received encouragement from her friends Jacques and Raïssa Maritain, both of whom had become Benedictine oblates, to affiliate with the Benedictine heritage. She formed her first connection with the English Benedictines at Portsmouth, Rhode Island, through her friend, Ade Bethune, who taught at the priory school. Dorothy was affiliated with Portsmouth from 1942 to 1946, but she became more particularly interested in St Procopius Abbey – Rembert Sorg's monastery and a centre for unity between the Eastern and Western Churches. She became a professed Benedictine oblate on 26 April 1955.[11] Dorothy's oblation grounded her in the Benedictine monastic tradition and helped to frame her spirituality. She formed a close friendship with another Benedictine oblate, Helene Iswolsky, who also worked on behalf of the unity between Eastern and Western Churches, notably through her 'Third Hour' discussion series, supported by Dorothy Day.

Dorothy also carried on a busy correspondence with Thomas Merton. Both were converts and writers who fought passionately for peace, non-violence and world justice. Dorothy published a number of Merton's articles in *The Catholic Worker*. She also knew another monastic connection in her relationship with the Jesus Caritas Fraternity of de Foucauld origin. Dorothy felt a keen affinity for de Foucauld, the simplicity of life among his 'Little Brothers' and 'Little Sisters' of Jesus, and their shared ministry to the poor. They inspired her to live her own charism with fervour, though she could never have disengaged from the world, as they ask of their lay affiliates. Dorothy would live her monastic oblation through her integration of prayer and work in the Catholic Worker movement.

During the 1940s, Dorothy Day became a frequent participant and active supporter of the retreat movement in the United States. She had already experimented with some retreat days of recollection sponsored by the Catholic Worker and given by people such as Fulton J. Sheen, Joachim Benson and Paul Hanly Furfey. When what became known as the Lacouture retreat movement began to spread in the United States, Dorothy became an enthusiastic supporter of its proponents, Pacifique Roy and John Hugo. Though both these men became controversial figures, Dorothy continued to support and sponsor their type of retreat in her Catholic Worker houses of hospitality, on the farm communes and, later, retreat houses. In 1943, Dorothy took a temporary leave from the Catholic Worker to experience some solitude and silence for a year. During this time she attended various retreats for women, spent time with her daughter in preparation for Tamar's marriage, lived in rural settings and wrote an occasional piece for *The Catholic Worker*. She decided to work to establish a retreat house at one of the Catholic Worker's farms. She worked to incorporate manual labour and silence into the retreats' daily schedules.[12] She personally made retreats throughout her life, but found many later experiences lacking time for the silence she promoted in the Catholic Worker retreats.

During childhood, Dorothy had a terror of silence, but that terror transformed into a love for silence as she matured. Jim Forest and Robert Ellsberg both relate how Dorothy would sometimes get exasperated by the noise in a Catholic Worker house and shout into the hallway: 'Holy Silence!' Dorothy's vocation demanded that she try to find moments of silence and respite in the course of a very busy day. In the midst of all the noise, activity and endless line of daily crises in a house of hospitality, Dorothy could write that, for one who practises, there is always silence in the midst of it all.[13] She knew a call to solitude that sharpened her spiritual perceptions, but her lifestyle allowed little time for solitude. So, she carefully guarded what solitude she did have. Daniel Berrigan, friend and fellow peace activist, wrote on behalf of Dorothy's love for solitude, of which few have taken account.[14]

Dorothy Day realised her own strong need for community. Sounding very much the Benedictine oblate-in-the-making she was, Dorothy wrote about the need for community, the togetherness of living, working and sharing, and the love of God and neighbour in communal life.[15] Healthy community life consists in a balance between solitude and interaction. The solitary aspect of Dorothy's life enabled her participation in community to be communion. Her spiritual practice included daily Eucharist, rosary, *lectio divina*, spiritual reading, keeping a journal, weekly confession and regular retreats. Dorothy worked at staying mindful of God's presence; she struggled towards ceaseless prayer and followed Br Lawrence's method of the practice of the presence of God.[16] Dorothy's love expanded to embrace all suffering and to recognise the universal bonds of humanity in God's presence.[17] What Dorothy Day did with her felt universality was an amazing, precious witness of love. She remains a powerful model for those who have an affinity for the monastic ethos of silence and solitude, but must find ways to live that affinity outside the usual haunts of monastic solitude – in the city street, ghetto, prison cell, picket line and noisy apartment building.

18. CHRISTIAN DE CHERGÉ: MARTYRDOM FOR THE WORLD

Born into old nobility to Guy and Monique de Chergé, Christian de Chergé was one of eight children, the second-eldest. When he was only five, the de Chergé family accompanied M. de Chergé to Algeria in 1942 and remained there until the end of the war. Christian was a gifted child, one for whom his parents foresaw – at least in retrospect – a church-related career. The de Chergé children enjoyed their three years in Algeria as a great adventure. Already then, Christian felt a deep respect and affinity for Muslim prayer. Decades later, he would write how grateful he felt to his mother for instilling in her children a respect for the prayer postures of Muslims.[1] Christian was closest to his devout mother, and remained so throughout his life.

The family returned to France in 1945. Christian attended school in the section of Paris where they resided, eventually deciding to enter seminary studies at the Seminaire des Carmes in 1956. Breaking away from studies in 1958 to fulfil his military obligation, Christian spent 1958–59 in France before serving as a commissioned officer in Algeria 1959–61. Christian was a young French officer in a country torn apart by civil strife and resenting anything connected with colonial France. Already then, Christian had become fascinated with the entire world of Islam. Everyone, though, did not appreciate his fascination. Christian had developed a friendship with a devout Algerian Muslim policeman Mohamed, who worked for the French authorities. Mohamed was the father of ten children. One day while he and Christian were walking through the streets of Algiers, they became involved in a scuffle with members of the anti-colonialist National Liberation Army who pointed their rifles at the young French officer whom Mohamed shielded with his body. Mohamed's mutilated dead body was discovered the next day – his price for protecting Christian and working for the French.

This episode became pivotal in Christian's life, for their friendship had grown to the point that they prayed for one another. Christian saw Mohamed as a martyr of love. His death became a focus of communion for Christian, communion of love in God. Later in life, Christian would look upon Mohamed as crucial for his lifelong pursuit of dialogue with Islam, because he had promised his dead friend to become simply a praying person among other praying people.[2] Out of this event, Christian would begin a progressive elaboration of his spirituality of dialogue and encounter. He now felt intimately tied to Algeria and intuited that his vocation would eventually place him back in that country.[3] After military service, he returned to his seminary studies. During the summers of 1961 and 1962, he participated in sessions regarding Islamic–Christian dialogue, based on the encounters experienced at the Benedictine monastery of Toumliline.

Christian de Chergé was ordained priest on 21 March 1964. Though he already sensed a monastic vocation, Archbishop (coadjutor) of Paris Venillot asked Christian to give five years to the Paris Church. From 1964 to 1969, Christian served as priest of Sacré Coeur in Montmartre, directing the parochial school attached to the basilica. He performed admirably at Montmartre, but after the requested five years, Christian turned to the task of becoming a monk. He chose the Trappist abbey of Notre Dame de'Aiguebelle, which had a daughter house in Algeria, Our Lady of Atlas (Tibhirine). Showing his firm intention already upon his entrance to monastic life, he wrote to a friend as he was leaving Paris that he was going to Algeria to pray with Muslims.[4] He became a novice at Aiguebelle in August 1969, and joined the Atlas monks in January 1971. Still a junior monk in August 1972, Christian found himself in Rome for two years of studies at the Pontifical

Institute for Arabic and Islamic Studies, during which time his love for the Koran and the Islamic spiritual tradition deepened.

Christian returned to Atlas in the summer of 1974. Even before the Order sent him to Rome for studies, many of the Atlas monks found themselves perplexed by Christian's devotion to Islamic spirituality and disturbed by his attempts to introduce some of it into the life of Tibhirine in the Atlas mountains. Christian renewed his temporary vows in both 1974 and 1975, but was accepted for solemn profession in 1976. Christian loved Tibhirine's silence, but he found the lack of support for encountering and dialoguing with Islam there frustrating and distressing. The monastery had, in fact, been questioning its presence at all in a Muslim country whose dissidents now wanted all foreigners out of the country. By allowing Christian's solemn vows with stability to Atlas, the Trappist community had come to grips with the dilemma and decided to fix stability in Algeria. In the truncated history of this monastery, Atlas had become a monastic presence of monks from various foreign houses living in Algeria, whereas from 1976 onwards Atlas monks had the opportunity of fixing their vows to Algerian soil.

Christian continued to push for the introduction of Islamic elements into the prayer life of Tibhirine, disturbing some monks who wrote letters of complaint to superiors back home. This ongoing tension within the community grew into a personal crisis for Christian who, in November 1979, travelled to Charles de Foucauld's former hermitage at Assekrem where he spent eight weeks in solitude, trying to decide whether to join the monastic Fraternity of Jerusalem who were more in tune with interreligious dialogue, or to remain a Trappist at Atlas. Christian returned to Tibhirine in January 1980, a reconfirmed Cistercian monk of Atlas. From then on, when the community atmosphere grew too stuffy, Christian would spend some solitary time at the nearby hermitage of Gationa, built on the mountainside facing Atlas/Tibhirine.[5] He found it difficult to compromise his positions on encountering Islam. Many were later to see in Christian another Charles de Foucauld, another 'Universal Brother'. In the autumn of 1980, Christian and his friend Claude Rault began a series of semi-annual meetings of Christian–Muslim encounter at Tibhirine known as the *ribât* (*ribât-es-salâm*, bond of peace). Outside the meetings, members strove to assimilate the fruits of dialogue by acts of love, pardon and communion against all violent forces.[6]

When the time arrived to elect a new superior, the Order had to face the fact that in a totally Muslim country the possibility for native vocations to the community was virtually non-existent. How could the Order re-establish an abbey there under such circumstances? Christian suggested that the house be lowered to the status of priory. He did this, Chenu writes, so that the monastery could be more a presence of people simply praying among others praying.[7] The priory of Tibhirine was so established and the community elected Christian prior in 1984. Under his priorship, the Atlas monks began to show more hospitality to Muslims – praying concurrently with local Muslims, working co-operatively with their Tibhirine neighbours, and including Islamic spirituality in their own Trappist monastic life.

Meanwhile, Islamic terrorist groups (FIS/Islamic Front of Salvation; AIS/Islamic Army of Salvation; GIA/Armed Islamic Group) stepped up their pressure to force foreigners and non-Muslims to leave Algeria. In an increasing pace of murders, members of the *ribât*, friends of the community and foreign religious were assassinated. The monks received their first lethal threat when the GIA just miles from the priory murdered fifteen Croatian workers. On 24 December 1993 Sayah Attia – the leader who had ordered the murders of the Croatians – visited the priory with demands for money, medical supplies, and the elderly monk who was a medical doctor. Christian refused the demands with justifications for his stance. Under the pall of terrorism, Christian had begun to write a testament explaining the community's position vis-à-vis Algeria, terrorism and martyrdom. On 1 January 1994 he finished the document and sent it privately to his youngest brother, Gerard, to be opened only upon Christian's death. On 27 March 1996 Christian de Chergé and six other Tibhirine monks were kidnapped, held in confinement for fifty-six days, and executed on 21 May 1996 because they were Christians, foreigners, and proponents of encounter and dialogue.

Due to the official communications sent by the terrorists to the French government in hope of obtaining freedom for jailed Islamic terrorists in exchange for the lives of the Trappist monks, the entire world learned of the senseless massacre of innocent, peace-loving monks who were actively seeking interreligious dialogue, friendship and reconciliation. Christian's brother, Gerard, on behalf of the de Chergé family, published Christian's testament, which was quickly publicised by the world press and various journals, three years after its composition. The world community was captivated by the story of Christian and his Trappist confrères caught in the vice of religious and political martyrdom. At a memorial service in Paris, Cardinal Jean-Marie Lustiger encouraged prayer that their death be a sign of hope and love.[8] Muslims everywhere joined their voices to protest the senseless murders. The Algerian President Bouteflika told the French National Assembly he must pay homage to the selflessness of the Algerian Church and its solidarity with humanity.[9]

Christian had once related in a homily how their Muslim neighbours desperately wanted the Trappists to remain at Tibhirine. One of their neighbours named Moussa told Christian that to leave would be to remove their own hope.[10] As the Cistercian General, Bernardo Olivera, wrote: the monks' decision to remain in a hostile Algeria was a sign of hope and peace for the universal Church, as well as their local Algerian Church.[11] The monks did not seek martyrdom; they made that position clear to everyone during their last three years in Algeria. They lived in terror, but the fear somehow knit them together more closely as a community of peace and sign of hope for others. They had already invested so much in their quiet life of dialogue and solidarity, they simply could not leave – even though each individual monk had that option.

The *ribât* had met at the monastery for years in order to seek areas of communion, such as those indicated by Christian in various ways over the years: ritual prayer, prayer of the heart, fasting, vigils, almsgiving, the communion of saints, a sense of praise and the pardon of God, and simple faith in the glory of the Totally Other. Christian saw these shared similarities as steps on a shared ascent.[12] The dialogue sponsored by the *ribât* continued after all the murders because the solidarity expressed by their Trappist brothers strengthened the resolve of remaining participants.[13] Through the personal charism and conviction of Christian de Chergé, the Trappists of Tibhirine had opened their doors to their Muslim neighbours. They had fashioned part of their monastery as a mosque, and both Christian and Muslim calls to prayer sounded out together. The monks had begun praying with an Arabic stance with hands outstretched in front of them. The Our Father was sung in Arabic, as were the Marian antiphons. They tried to be as inclusive as possible. Muslims were welcomed into prayer and into the monastery guesthouse, provided they respected the monastic silence and solitude.[14] At Poyo, Spain, Christian had explained the Atlas approach to his fellow Cistercian monks and nuns gathered in General Chapter – how hospitality had become their most important way to relate and share.[15]

This mutual sharing at Tibhirine also extended to the land and their livelihood. The monks shared the labour and produce of their extensive gardens by sharing the ownership of such with their Muslim neighbours. Likewise, the monks took part in the local village co-operative. The community stocked a medical dispensary where Brother Luke, a medical doctor, treated all who came. Once again, Christian explained their communal uniqueness at the Poyo Chapter by stating that the trust and loyalty demanded by their neighbours was a precious gift to the community.[16] Christian de Chergé led his community deeply towards union and communion because he felt it his destiny to do so. That is not too strong a description of his inner quest. Christian himself universalised this quest by saying that love knows no boundaries and the mercy surrounding love embraces all humanity.[17] Christian was a prophet who constantly pushed the limits of restraints because he passionately envisioned a truly universal Church.[18] He did so, along with his Trappist confrères, as an eloquent sign of peace, fellowship and dialogue in the midst of human conflict – fraught with terror, inhumane cruelty, and the spectre of forced exclusivity. Their testament is one of love and martyrdom for the world.

PART FIVE: SOLITUDE AND THE HUMAN FAMILY

19. CONCLUSION: THE 'MONK WITHIN' AND UNIVERSAL SOLIDARITY

My purpose in writing this book has been to highlight the more salient factors involved in the formation of monastic solitude in its various hues. I have not tried to represent all of the monastic variations on this theme. For instance, I could have devoted space to the Gilbertines, the hermits of Grand-mont, the Celestines, Olivetans and other generically Benedictine groups, but chose to concentrate on the more widely recognised movements. I could also have explored soli-tude lived among the mendicants, especially among Franciscan, Augustinian and Carmelite friars' eremitical tra-ditions, but I decided to restrict my survey to the monastic world. This focus has allowed space for the investigation of contemporary examples of solitaries who were connected to the monastic ethos and who have prophetically lived their calls to solitude in ways that clearly spoke a language of univer-sality and solidarity with the human family.

Such language is not at all new to the world of monastic solitude. Any healthy religious solitude with silence that truly listens to the Word will reach out universally to all people, all life and creation, without bracketing spheres of intolerance or creating psychological ghettos of isolation. Monastic solitude speaks love and peace to the heart of humanity. There are those who say that every human being has a 'monk within'. Raimundo Panikkar, for example, asserts that the 'monk' archetype is part of who we are as human beings trying to integrate our lives around the centre of all being.[1]

We are all drawn inward, towards the centre of existence. We come to know ourselves as drawn into a presence. Solitude ushers us into presence, towards which the language of silence is most attentive. If we find ourselves in relation to that presence at the centre of our being, we will move our hearts, indeed our lives, outwardly in solidarity with all our brothers and sisters throughout the world, universally, without exception. The deeper the contemplative communion, the wider the embrace in solidarity. Solitude teaches us, after all, that we are really brothers and sisters of the same family. This is the great gift that the 'monk within' offers the world – human solidarity, universally expressed in communion with God. And a great irony rests within this gift. Authentically lived, monastic solitude breaks through human barriers of isolation and speaks a silent word of universal love and solidarity with all life.

NOTES

ABBREVIATIONS USED

ABR   *American Benedictine Review*
CC   *Collectanea Cisterciensia*
CSQ   *Cistercian Studies Quarterly*
DS   *Dictionnaire de Spiritualité*
FOTC   *Fathers of the Church (Series title, published by the Catholic University of America)*
MS   *Monastic Studies*
RR   *Review for Religious*
SM   *Studia Monastica*
VM   *Vita Monastica*
VS   *La Vie Spirituelle*
SVSP   St Vladimir's Seminary Press
WS   *Word and Spirit*

1: INTRODUCTION: THE SILENT COMMUNION OF SOLITUDE

1. See John Paul Blanchard, 'A Riddle of Loneliness: A Theological Reading of the Contemporary Reality, its Meaning and Challenge', *ABR* 42:4 (1991), 391.
2. See Michael Casey, 'Solitariness', *Tjurunga* 33 (1987), 3.
3. See Blanchard, 'Riddle', 401.
4. Blanchard, 'Riddle', 405.
5. See Jean Leclercq, *Aux Sources de la Spiritualité Occidentale* (Paris: Cerf, 1964), p. 222.
6. See Jean Guitton, 'Solitude and Silence', *MS* 2 (1964), 48.
7. See Leclercq, *Aux Sources*, p. 222.
8. See Henri van Cranenburgh, 'Pour une revalorisation de la cellule', *CC* 38:1 (1976), 25.
9. Peter-Damian Belisle, 'The "Hermit" Archetype within the Monastic Spiritual Journey', *WS* 15 (1993), 44.
10. Belisle, 'The "Hermit" Archetype', 48.
11. See Pierre-Yves Emery, 'Solitude et communion', *CC* 40:1 (1978), 26–7.

12. See Casey, 'Solitariness', 3.
13. See Ambrose Wathen, *Silence: The Meaning of Silence in the Rule of St Benedict* (Washington DC: Cistercian Publications, 1973), p. xii.
14. See Max Picard, *The World of Silence* (South Bend IN: Regnery/Gateway, 1952), p. 24.
15. See Jean Leclercq, 'Silence et parole dans l'expérience spirituelle d'hier et d'aujourd'hui', *CC* 45 (1983), 195.
16. See Guitton, 'Solitude', 49.
17. See Kallistos Ware, 'Silence in Prayer: The Meaning of *Hesychia*', *One Yet Two: Monastic Tradition East and West*, ed. B. Pennington (Kalamazoo MI: Cistercian Publications, 1976), p. 30.
18. See Wathen, *Silence*, p. 231.
19. See Ware, 'Silence', 26.
20. See Picard, *World*, p. 227.
21. See David Ranson, 'The Experience of Silence in the Christian Monastic Heart', *Tjurunga* 55 (1998), 41.

2: FIGURES OF OLD TESTAMENT SOLITUDE

1. See David Daiches, *Moses: The Man and His Vision* (New York: Praeger, 1975), p. 173.
2. See Divo Barsotti, *La Spiritualité de L'Exode* (Paris: Téqui, 1982), p. 41.
3. See Elie Wiesel, 'The Loneliness of Moses', *Loneliness*, ed. Rouner (Notre Dame IN: University of Notre Dame Press, 1998), p. 136.
4. See Dewey M. Beegle, *Moses, The Servant of Yahweh* (Grand Rapids MI: Eerdmans, 1972), p. 80.
5. See Paul-Marie Guillaume, 'Moïse', *DS* 10c (1979), 1469–70.
6. See Wiesel, 'Loneliness', p.138.
7. See Martin Buber, *Moses: the Revelation and the Covenant* (New York: Harper & Row, 1958), p. 201.
8. See Elie Wiesel, *Five Biblical Portraits* (Notre Dame IN: University of Notre Dame Press, 1981), p. 39.
9. See Jean Leclercq, *The Love of Learning and the Desire for God* (New York: Fordham University Press, 1961), p. 106; see also Ann E. Matter, *The Voice of My Beloved: The* Song of Songs *in Western Medieval Christianity* (Philadelphia: University of Pennsylvania Press, 1990), p. 6.
10. See Leclercq, *Love*, p. 108.
11. See Bernard of Clairvaux, *On the Song of Songs* I (Spencer MA: Cistercian Publications, 1971), Sermon 1.11, quoted by M. C. Halflants in 'Introduction', p. x.
12. See William E. Phipps, 'The Plight of the *Song of Songs*', *The Song of Songs*, ed. H. Bloom (New York: Chelsea House, 1988), p. 14; see also Marvin Pope, *Song of Songs* (New York: Doubleday, 1977), p. 123.

13. See Paul Verdeyen and Raffaele Fassetta, 'Introduction', Bernard de Clairvaux, *Sermons sur Le Cantique* (Paris: Cerf, 1996), p. 53.
14. See Bernard of Clairvaux, *Sermons on the Song of Songs*, Sermon 84.7, quoted by Michael Casey, *Athirst For God: Spiritual Desire in Bernard of Clairvaux's* Sermons on the Song of Songs (Kalamazoo MI: Cistercian Publications, 1988), p. 53.
15. See Casey, *Athirst*, p. 317.
16. See Roland E. Murphy, *The Song of Songs* (Minneapolis MN: Fortress Press, 1990), p. 25.

3: FIGURES OF NEW TESTAMENT SOLITUDE

1. See Jean Daniélou, *The Work of John the Baptist* (Baltimore: Helicon, 1966), p. 12.
2. See John Cassian, *The Conferences* (New York: Newman, 1997), p. 639.
3. See G. Penco, 'S. Giovanni Battista nel ricordo del monachesimo medievale', *SM* 3 (1961), 20–9.
4. See Edward Malatesta, 'Jesus and Loneliness', *The Way* (1976), p. 248.
5. See Cassian, *Conferences*, p. 375.
6. See William Reiser, 'Christology and the Solitary Life', *RR* 39 (1980), 714.
7. See Louis Bouyer, 'The Blessed Virgin Mary and Christian Monasticism', *WS* 10 (1988), 36–7.
8. See Elizabeth A. Johnson, 'Marian Devotion in the Western Church', *Christian Spirituality II: High Middle Ages and Reformation*, ed. J. Raitt (New York: Crossroad, 1989), p. 392.
9. See Domiciano Fernandez and Theodore Koehler, 'Marie (Sainte Vierge)', *DS* 10 (1977), 451.
10. Fernandez and Koehler, 'Marie', 452.

4: SOLITUDE IN ATHANASIUS' *LIFE OF ANTONY*

1. See H. Weingarten, *Ursprung des Mönchtums im nach konstantinischen Zeitalter* (Gotha, 1877).
2. See Samuel Rubenson, *The Letters of St Antony: Origenist Theology, Monastic Tradition and the Making of a Saint* (Lund: University Press, 1990).
3. See G. J. M. Bartelink, 'Introduction', Athanase D'Alexandrie, *Vie D'Antoine* (Paris: Cerf, 1994).
4. See *The Letters of St Antony the Great*, tr. D. Chitty (Oxford: SLG Press, 1975), p. 5.
5. See Étienne Bettencourt, 'L'ideal religieux de Saint Antoine et son actualité', *Antonius Magnus Eremita*, ed. B. Steidle (Rome: Herder, 1956), 47–58.

6. See *The Sayings of the Desert Fathers: The Alphabetical Collection*, tr. B. Ward (London: Mowbray, 1975), p. 2.
7. *Sayings*, p. 2.
8. See Athanasius, *The Life of Antony and the Letter to Marcellinus*, tr. R. C. Gregg (Mahwah NJ: Paulist Press, 1980), ch. 69.
9. Athanasius, *Life*, ch. 75.
10. See Louis Bouyer, *La Vie de S. Antoine* (Bellefontaine: Fontenelle, 1977), pp. 116–17.
11. See Athanasius, *Life*, ch. 42.
12. See *The Letters of Ammonas, Successor of Saint Antony*, ed. S. Brock, tr. D. Chitty (Oxford: SLG Press, 1979), p. 16.
13. *Ammonas*, p. 16.
14. *Ammonas*, p. 16.
15. See Jean Leclercq, 'Saint Antoine dans la tradition monastique médiévale', *Antonius Magnus Eremita*, ed. B. Steidle (Rome: Herder, 1956), p. 235.
16. Leclercq, 'Saint Antoine', p. 236.

5: DESERT SOLITUDE: *LIVES* AND *SAYINGS* OF DESERT SOLITARIES

1. See Benedicta Ward, 'Introduction', *Lives of the Desert Fathers*, tr. N. Russell (Kalamazoo MI: Cistercian Publications, 1980), p. 3, quoting additions to the text by Rufinus.
2. See *Lives of the Desert Fathers*, p. 69.
3. See *The Sayings of the Desert Fathers: The Alphabetical Collection*, tr. B. Ward (Oxford: Mowbray, 1975), p. 75.
4. See *Lives of the Desert Fathers*, p. 62.
5. See Evagrius Ponticus, *The Praktikos, Chapters on Prayer* (Spencer MA: Cistercian Publications, 1970), p. 29.
6. This is not Didymus the Blind.
7. See *Lives of the Desert Fathers*, p. 106.
8. *Lives of the Desert Fathers*, p. 68.
9. See *Sayings of the Desert Fathers*, p. 65.
10. See *The World of the Desert Fathers*, tr. C. Stewart (Kalamazoo MI: Cistercian Publications, 1986), p. 35.
11. See Susanna Elm, 'Virgins of God' (Oxford: Clarendon Press, 1994), p. 263.
12. See Owen Chadwick (ed.), *The Sayings of the Desert Fathers* in *Western Asceticism* (Philadelphia: Westminster Press, 1958), p. 43.
13. See *The Wisdom of the Desert Fathers: The Apophthegmata Patrum' (The Anonymous Series)*, tr. B. Ward (Oxford: SLG Press, 1975), p. xiii.
14. See *Sayings of the Desert Fathers*, pp. 22, 118.
15. *Sayings of the Desert Fathers*, p. 152.
16. *Sayings of the Desert Fathers*, p. 69.

17. *Sayings of the Desert Fathers*, p. 191.
18. *Sayings of the Desert Fathers*, p. 88.

6: SOLITUDE IN SELECTED MONASTIC PATRISTIC SOURCES

1. See Augustine Holmes, *A Life Pleasing to God: The Spirituality of the Rules of St Basil* (London: Darton, Longman & Todd, 2000), p. 27.
2. See St Basil, *Letters*, Vol. II, tr. A. Way (New York: FOTC, 1955), p. 128.
3. See St Basil, *Ascetical Works*, tr. M. Wagner (Washington DC: Catholic University of America Press, 1962), p. 245.
4. See St Basil, *Letters*, Vol. I, tr. A. Way (Washington DC: Catholic University of America Press, 1951), pp. 6–7.
5. Basil, *Letters* I, p. 47.
6. See Basil, *Ascetical*, pp. 248–52.
7. See Basil, *Letters* I, p. 5.
8. See Evagrius Ponticus, *The Mind's Long Journey to the Holy Trinity; The 'Ad Monachos'*, tr. J. Driscoll (Collegeville MN: Liturgical Press, 1992), p. 33.
9. See Evagrius Ponticus, *The Praktikos, Chapters on Prayer*, tr. J. E. Bamberger (Spencer MA: Cistercian Publications, 1970), p. 20.
10. Evagrius Ponticus, *Praktikos*, p. 20.
11. See Gabriel Bunge, *Akedia il male oscuro* (Magnano: Qiqajon, 1999), p. 113 (*Sententiae ad virginem*).
12. Bunge, Akedia, p. 149 (*The Praktikos* # 124).
13. See Holmes, *A Life*, p. 149.
14. See Louis Bouyer, *The Spirituality of the New Testament and the Fathers* (New York: Desclée, 1960), p. 381.
15. See Jean-Jacques Antier, *Lérins, l'île sainte de la Côte d'Azur* (Paris: Editions S.O.S., 1973), p. 133; see also Léon Cristiani, 'Introduction', Eucher De Lyon, *Du Mépris du Monde* (Paris: Nouvelles Editions Latines, 1950), p. 12.
16. See Ivan Gobry, *Les Moines en Occident*, Vol. II (Paris: Fayard, 1985), p. 258.
17. See Eucher of Lyons, 'In Praise of the Desert', tr. C. Cummings, *CSQ* 11 (1976), 60.
18. Eucher, 'Praise', 69.
19. Eucher, 'Praise', 69.
20. Eucher, 'Praise', 70.
21. See Michel Olphe-Galliard, 'Cassien (Jean)' *DS* II (1953), 222.
22. See John Cassian, *The Conferences*, tr. B. Ramsey (New York: Newman, 1997), pp. 29–31.
23. Cassian, *Conferences*, p. 639.
24. Cassian, *Conferences*, p. 677.
25. See John Cassian, *The Institutes*, tr. B. Ramsey (New York: Newman, 2000), p. 138.

26. Cassian, *Institutes*, p. 201.
27. See Theodoret of Cyrrhus, *A History of the Monks of Syria*, tr. R. Price (Kalamazoo MI: Cistercian Publications, 1985), p. 51.
28. See John Binns, *Ascetics and Ambassadors of Christ: The Monasteries of Palestine 314–631* (Oxford: Clarendon Press, 1994), pp. 100–2.
29. See Derwas J. Chitty, *The Desert a City* (Crestwood NY: SVSP, 1995), p. 48.
30. See Cyril of Scythopolis, *Lives of the Monks of Palestine*, tr. R. Price (Kalamazoo MI: Cistercian Publications, 1991), p.104.
31. See Yīzhar Hirschfeld, *The Judean Desert Monasteries in the Byzantine Period* (New Haven CT: Yale University Press, 1992), p. 20.
32. See John Climacus, *The Ladder of Divine Ascent*, tr. C. Luibheid and N. Russell (New York: Paulist Press, 1982), p. 148.
33. See Kallistos Ware, 'Introduction', John Climacus, *Ladder*, p. 50.
34. See Isaac the Syrian, *The Wisdom of Saint Isaac the Syrian*, tr. S. Brock (Oxford: SLG Press, 1997), p. 1.
35. The two sources for Isaac's biographical details are: Isho 'denah's 'The Book of Chastity', ed. J. Chabot, *Mélanges d'Archéologie et d'Histoire* 16 (1846), 277–8; an anonymous West-Syrian source, ed. I. Rahmani, *Studia Syriaca* I (1904), pp. 32–3.
36. See Élie Khalifé-Hachem, 'Isaac De Nineve', *DS* 7 (1971), 2042.
37. See Sebastian Brock, 'St Isaac of Nineveh', *Sobornost* 7 (1975), 81.
38. See Hilarion Alfeyev, *The Spiritual World of Isaac the Syrian* (Kalamazoo MI: Cistercian Publications, 2000), p. 61.
39. See Isaac the Syrian, *Wisdom*, p. 14.
40. See Alfeyev, *Spiritual*, p. 88.
41. See Isaac the Syrian, *Wisdom*, pp. 11–12.

7: SOLITUDE IN BENEDICT OF NURSIA

1. See Gregory the Great, *The Life of Saint Benedict*, tr. H. Costello and E. Bhaldraithe (Petersham: St Bede's Publications, 1993), p. 3.
2. See Peter Anson, *The Call of the Desert* (London: SPCK, 1964), p. 63.

8: CAMALDOLESE BENEDICTINE SOLITUDE: THE LAURA

1. A major portion of this chapter appeared originally in *The Privilege of Love: Camaldolese Benedictine Spirituality*, ed. P. D. Belisle (Collegeville MN: The Liturgical Press). Permission is granted by the Order of St Benedict.
2. Bruno of Querfurt, *The Life of the Five Brothers* in Thomas Matus (tr. and ed.), *The Mystery of Romuald and the Five Brothers* (Trabuco Canyon: Source Books, 1994), p. 95.
3. Bruno, *Life*, in Matus, *Mystery*, p. 91.
4. Peter Damian, *The Life of Blessed Romuald* in Matus, *Mystery*, p. 182.

5. See Jean Leclercq, *Saint Pierre Damien, Ermite et Homme D'Église* (Roma: Edizioni di Storia e Letteratura, 1960), p. 30.

6. Matus, *Mystery*, p. 188.

7. Matus, *Mystery*, p. 158.

8. See Peter Damian, 'Letter 50' in *Letters 31–60*, tr. O. Blum (Washington DC: Catholic University of America Press, 1990), p. 291.

9. See Peter Damian, 'Letter 28' in *Letters 1–30*, tr. O. Blum (Washington DC: Catholic University of America Press, 1989), p. 262.

10. Peter Damian, *Letters 1–30*, p. 265.

11. See André Louf, 'Solitudo Pluralis' in *Solitude and Communion: Papers on the Hermit Life* (Oxford: SLG Press, 1977), p. 22.

12. Rudulphus Camaldulensis, *Constitutiones* in *Annales Camaldulenses Ordinis Sancti Benedicti*, 9 vols, ed. J.-B. Mittarelli (Venetiae, 1755–1773), III, App., col. 529.

13. *Annales*, p. 527.

14. *Annales*, p. 532.

15. *Annales*, p. 533.

16. *Annales*, p. 533.

17. See Giovanni Tabacco, '*Privilegium amoris*: aspetti della spiritualità Romualdina' in *Spiritualità e Cultura nel Medioevo* (Napoli: Liguori, 1993), p. 177.

18. See Paolo Giustiniani, *Regola Della vita Eremitica* (Seregno: Abbazia San Benedetto, 1996), p. 73.

19. Giustiniani, *Regola*, p. 77.

20. Giustiniani, *Regola*, p. 94.

21. See Paul Giustiniani, 'De l'institution plus parfaite de la réclusion', *CC* 54 (1992), 93.

22. See Giustiniani, *Regola*, p. 35.

23. See Innocenzo Gargano, 'Introduzione' in Benedetto Calati, *Sapienza Monastica* (Roma: Studia Anselmiana, 1994); see also Innocenzo Gargano, *Camaldolesi nella Spiritualità Italiana del Novecento* I (Bologna: Edizioni Dehoniane Bologna, 2000).

24. Gargano, *Camaldolesi*, p. 43.

25. Anselmo Giabbani, 'Spirito camaldolese', *VM* 58 (1959), 100.

26. Anselmo Giabbani, *L'Eremo: Vita e spiritualità Eremitica nel Monachesimo Camaldolese Primitivo* (Brescia: Morcelliana, 1945), p. 231.

9: CARTHUSIAN SOLITUDE: *ALONE* TOGETHER

1. See A Carthusian, *The Way of Silent Love: Carthusian Novice Conferences* (Kalamazoo MI: Cistercian Publications/London: Darton, Longman & Todd, 1993), p. 90.

2. Carthusian, *Way*, p. 97.

3. See Bernard Bligny, 'L'Érémitisme et Les Chartreux' in *L'Eremitismo in Occidente nei Secoli XI e XII* (Milano: Vita e Pensiero, 1965), p. 261.

4. Anon., 'La Spiritualità Certosina' *VM* 62 (1960), 133.
5. Anon., 'La Spiritualiti', 136.
6. See Anon., *The Wound of Love: A Carthusian Miscellany* (Kalamazoo MI: Cistercian Publications/London: Darton, Longman & Todd, 1994), p. 28.
7. Anon., *Wound*, p. 46.
8. Anon., *Wound*, p. 61.
9. Anon., 'La Spiritualità', 132.
10. Anon., *Wound*, p. 31.
11. Anon., *Wound*, p. 52.
12. Carthusian, *Way*, p. 35.
13. Gordon Mursell points out that two of Bruno's original companions were canons of Saint-Ruf. See Gordon Mursell, *The Theology of the Carthusian Life in the Writings of St Bruno and Guigo I* (Salzburg: Universitat, 1988), Introduction.
14. See Un Chartreux, 'Introduction' in Guigues 1er, *Les Méditations* (Paris: Cerf, 1983), p. 36.
15. See Guigues 1er, *Coutumes de Chartreuse* (Paris: Cerf, 1984), p. 233.
16. Guigues 1er, *Coutumes*, p. 197.
17. Guigues 1er, *Coutumes*, p. 197.
18. See Guigo II, *The Ladder of Monks* (New York: Doubleday, 1978), p. 89.
19. See Guigo II, *Twelve Meditations* (New York: Doubleday, 1978), pp. 104–5.
20. See André Ravier, *Dom Augustin Guillerand, Prieur Chartreux 1877–1945* (Bruges: Desclée, 1965), p. 50.
21. Both *Carthusian Silence* and *Carthusian Speech* were published in one English volume, *They Speak By Silences* (London: Longmans, Green & Co. Ltd, 1955; reprinted Darton, Longman & Todd, 1996).
22. See A Carthusian, *They Speak*, p. 75.
23. Carthusian, *They Speak*, p. 1.
24. Carthusian, *They Speak*, p. 131.
25. Carthusian, *They Speak*, p. 5.

10: CISTERCIAN SOLITUDE: ALONE *TOGETHER*

1. See Michael Casey, 'The Dialectic of Solitude and Communion in Cistercian Communities', *CS* 23:4 (1988), 293.
2. See Benedicta Ward, 'The Desert Myth' in *One Yet Two: Monastic Tradition East and West*, ed. B. Pennington (Kalamazoo MI: Cistercian Publications, 1976), p. 194.
3. See Casey, 'Dialectic', 300.
4. William of St-Thierry writes that Bernard was twenty-three when he became a monk in 1113.
5. Jean Leclercq, 'St Bernard of Clairvaux and the Contemplative Community', *CSQ*, 7:2 (1972), 139.

6. See S. Bernardus, *Sermones* III, ed. J. Leclercq and H. Rochais (Rome: Editiones Cistercienses, 1970), p. 258 (Sermon # 42).
7. See Leclercq, 'St Bernard', 99–100; see n. 7, p. 100.
8. See William of St-Thierry et al., *St Bernard of Clairvaux (Vita Prima Bernardi)* (Westminster MD: Newman Press, 1966), p. 14.
9. See Bernard of Clairvaux, *On the Song of Songs* III (Kalamazoo MI: Cistercian Publications, 1979), p. 172.
10. See Bernard of Clairvaux, *On the Song of Songs* IV (Kalamazoo MI: Cistercian Publications, 1979), p. 213.
11. See Patrick Ryan, 'The Witness of William of St Thierry to the Spirit and Aims of the Early Cistercians', *The Cistercian Spirit*, ed. B. Pennington (Spencer MA: Cistercian Publications, 1970), p. 234.
12. See William of St-Thierry, *St Bernard*, pp. 58, 66.
13. See William of St-Thierry, *The Golden Epistle* (Kalamazoo MI: Cistercian Publications, 1976), p. 22.
14. See John J. Conley, 'The Eremitical Anthropology of William of St-Thierry', *CSQ* 25 (1990), 116.
15. See Thomas Merton, *Day of a Stranger* (Salt Lake City UT: Gibbs M. Smith, 1981), pp. 31–3.
16. See Thomas Merton, *Contemplation in a World of Action* (Garden City NY: Image Books, 1973), p. 315.
17. Merton, *Contemplation*, p. 330.
18. See Thomas Merton, *Thoughts in Solitude* (New York: Dell, 1958), p. 148.

11: ANCHORETIC SOLITUDE: JULIAN OF NORWICH

1. See Hugh Farmer (ed.), 'Introduction', *The Monk of Farne* (Baltimore: Helicon, 1961), p. 9.
2. See Rotha Mary Clay, *The Hermits and Anchorites of England* (London: Methuen, 1914), p. 171.
3. See Ann K. Warren, *Anchorites and Their Patrons in Medieval England* (Berkeley: University of California Press, 1985), p. 2.
4. Warren, *Anchorites*, p. 289.
5. See Anne Savage and Nicholas Watson, 'General Introduction' in *Anchoretic Spirituality* (New York: Paulist Press, 1991), p. 19.
6. See Warren, *Anchorites*, p. 29.
7. See Grace M. Jantzen, *Julian of Norwich* (New York: Paulist Press/London: SPCK, 1988), p. 33.
8. See Edmund Colledge and James Walsh, 'Introduction', Julian of Norwich, *Showings* (New York: Paulist Press, 1978), p. 20.
9. See Jean Leclercq, 'Preface', Julian of Norwich, *Showings*, p. 11.

12: THE RUSSIAN *STARETS*: SERAPHIM OF SAROV

1. See Thomas Merton, 'Preface' in S. Bolshakoff, *Russian Mystics* (Kalamazoo MI: Cistercian Publications, 1977), p. xv.
2. See Kallistos Ware, *The Inner Kingdom* (Crestwood NY: SVSP, 2001).
3. See Merton, 'Preface', p. xii.
4. See Vsévolod Rochcau, *Saint Séraphim: Sarov et Divéyevo* (Bellefontaine: Spiritualité Occidentale, 1987), p. 21.

13: STARETS SILOUANE OF ATHOS: COMPASSION FOR ALL

1. See Maxime Egger, 'Starets Silouane, un saint actuel et universel', *Contacts* 171 (1995), 165.
2. See Archimandrite Sophrony, *The Monk of Mount Athos: Starets Silouane 1866–1938* (Crestwood NY: SVSP, 1973), p. 28.
3. Sophrony, *Monk*, p. 93.
4. See Olivier Clément, 'Quelques notes sur la spiritualité du starets Silouane', *Contacts* 184 (1998), 292.
5. See Christian Portier, 'L'amour au coeur du monde et de l'Église: Thérèse de Lisieux, Silouane de l'Athos', *Contacts* 37 (1985), 21.
6. See Sophrony, *Monk*, p. 94.

14: CHARLES DE FOUCAULD: THE UNIVERSAL BROTHER

1. See Ali Merad, *Christian Hermit in an Islamic World: A Muslim's View of Charles de Foucauld*, tr. Z. Hersov (New York: Paulist Press, 1999), pp. 74–5.
2. See Jean-François Six, *Spiritual Autobiography of Charles de Foucauld,* tr. J. Smith (Denville: Dimension, 1964), p. 147.
3. See Charles de Foucauld, *Meditations of a Hermit*, tr. C. Balfour (New York: Orbis Books, 1981), p. 177.
4. De Foucauld, *Meditations*, p. 47.
5. De Foucauld, *Meditations*, p. 76.
6. See J.-F. Six, 'Frère Universel', *VS* 533 (1966), 657.
7. See Peter France, *Hermits: The Insights of Solitude* (New York: St Martins, 1996), p. 150.
8. See Merad, *Christian*, pp. 20–1.
9. See Jean-François Six, 'Foucauld (Charles de)', *DS* 5 (1963), 730.

15: JULES MONCHANIN: PASSION FOR THE UNIVERSAL

1. See Jules Monchanin, *In Quest of the Absolute: The Life and Work of Jules Monchanin*, ed. J. Weber (Kalamazoo MI: Cistercian Publications, 1977), p. 16.
2. Monchanin, *Quest*, p. 22.
3. Monchanin, *Quest*, p. 105.

4. Monchanin, *Quest*, p. 27.

5. See Bede Griffiths, 'Preface' in Monchanin, *Quest*, p. 2.

6. See Françoise Jacquin, 'The Spiritual Journey of Jules Monchanin, or A Passion for the Universal', *Jules Monchanin (1895–1957) as Seen from East and West I: Lyon – Fleurie* (Delhi: ISPCK, 2001), p. 135.

7. See Jacquin, 'Spiritual', p. 139.

8. See Monchanin, *Quest*, p. 34.

9. See J. Monchanin and Henri Le Saux, *Ermites du Saccidananda* (Paris: Casterman, 1956), p. 121.

10. Monchanin and Le Saux, *Ermites*, p. 122.

11. Monchanin and Le Saux, *Ermites*, p. 166.

12. See Monchanin, *Quest*, p. 23.

13. Monchanin, *Quest*, pp. 34, 57.

14. See Monchanin and Le Saux, *Ermites*, p. 113.

15. Monchanin and Le Saux, *Ermites*, pp. 129, 130; also see Monchanin, *Quest*, pp. 31, 121.

16. Monchanin, *Quest*, p. 76.

17. See Françoise Jacquin, *Jules Monchanin prêtre 1895–1957* (Paris: Cerf, 1996).

18. See Jacquin, 'Spiritual', p. 130.

16. CATHERINE DE HUECK DOHERTY: THE LITTLE MANDATE

1. See Catherine de Hueck Doherty, *Fragments of My Life* (Notre Dame IN: Ave Maria Press, 1979), pp. 76–7.

2. Doherty, *Fragments*, p. 95.

3. Doherty, *Fragments*, p. 111.

4. Doherty, *Fragments*, p. 172.

5. See Catherine de Hueck Doherty, *Sobornost* (Notre Dame IN: Ave Maria Press, 1977), p. 91.

6. See Catherine de Hueck Doherty, *The Gospel without Compromise* (Notre Dame IN: Ave Maria Press, 1976), p. 144.

7. Doherty, *Gospel*, p. 145.

8. See Catherine de Hueck Doherty, *Poustinia* (Notre Dame IN: Ave Maria Press, 1975), p. 207.

9. See Doherty, *Gospel*, pp. 124, 125, 145; also see Catherine de Hueck Doherty, *Doubts, Loneliness, Rejection* (New York: Alba House, 1981), p. 59.

10. See Doherty, *Poustinia*, p. 206.

11. Doherty, *Poustinia*, p. 64.

12. Doherty, *Poustinia*, p. 66.

13. See Catherine de Hueck Doherty, *Molchanie: The Silence of God* (New York: Crossroad, 1982), p. 16.

14. See Doherty, *Gospel*, p. 59.

15. See Doherty, *Poustinia*, p. 69.

16. Doherty, *Poustinia*, p. 213.

17: DOROTHY DAY: SOLIDARITY WITH THE POOR

1. See Dorothy Day, *Selected Writings; By Little and By Little*, ed. R. Ellsberg (Maryknoll NY: Orbis Books, 1992), p. 352.
2. See Robert Ellsberg, 'Introduction' in Day, *Selected Writings*, p. xx.
3. See Dorothy Day, *The Long Loneliness* (San Francisco: Harper, 1980), p. 166.
4. See Marc Ellis, 'The Legacy of Peter Maurin', *Cross Currents* 34 (1984), 295.
5. Day, *Long*, p. 237.
6. See Brigid O'Shea Merriman, *Searching For Christ: The Spirituality of Dorothy Day* (Notre Dame IN: University of Notre Dame Press, 1994), p. 102. I am deeply grateful to Merriman's book, especially chapter 3, 'The Impact of Monasticism'.
7. See Dorothy Day, *On Pilgrimage* (Grand Rapids MI: Eerdmans, 1999), p. 115.
8. See Jim Forest, *Love is the Measure: A Biography of Dorothy Day* (Maryknoll NY: Orbis Books, 1994), p. 156.
9. See Merriman, *Searching*, p. 107.
10. See Ellsberg, 'Introduction', p. xli.
11. See Merriman, *Searching*, p. 106; also see the May 1955 issue of *The Catholic Worker*.
12. Merriman, *Searching*, p. 149.
13. See Margaret and Michael Quigley, *The Dorothy Day Book* (Springfield: Templegate, 1982), p. 121; also see Dorothy Day, *Meditations*, ed. S. Vishnewski (New York: Paulist Press, 1970), p. 68.
14. See Daniel Berrigan, 'The Long Loneliness of Dorothy Day' in *Loneliness*, ed. L. Rounder (Notre Dame IN: University of Notre Dame Press, 1998), p. 164.
15. See Day, *Long*, p. 243.
16. See Day, *On Pilgrimage*, pp. 79, 110.
17. See Day, *Selected*, p. 9.

18: CHRISTIAN DE CHERGÉ: MARTYRDOM FOR THE WORLD

1. See Bernardo Olivera, 'Monk, Martyr, and Mystic: Christian de Chergé (1937–1996)', *CSQ* 34:3 (1999), 332.
2. See Marie-Christine Ray, *Christian de Chergé, prieur de Tibhirine* (Paris: Bayard, 1998), p. 85.
3. See Olivera, 'Monk', 323.
4. See Ray, *Christian*, p. 73.
5. Ray, *Christian*, pp. 139–40.
6. See Bruno Chenu (ed.), *Sept vies pour Dieu et L'Algérie* (Paris: Bayard, 1996), p. 50, quoting from the 'Propositions' of the *ribât-es-Sakâm*.
7. Chenu, *Sept vies*, p. 6.

8. See John W. Kiser, *The Monks of Tibhirine: Faith, Love, and Terror in Algeria* (New York: St Martin's, 2002), p. 234.
9. Kiser, *Monks*, p. 286.
10. See Robert Masson, *Tibhirine, Les Veilleurs de l'Atlas* (Paris: Cerf, 1998), p. 17.
11. See Bernardo Olivera, *How Far to Follow? The Martyrs of Atlas* (Petersham: St Bede's Publications, 1997), p. 47.
12. See Christian de Chergé, *L'Invincible Espérance*, ed. B. Chenu (Paris: Bayard, 1997), p. 179.
13. See Donald McGlynn, 'Atlas Martyrs', *CSQ* 32:2 (1997), 172.
14. See Christian de Chergé, *L'Invincible*, p. 190.
15. See Kiser, *Monks*, p. 133.
16. Kiser, *Monks*, p. 133.
17. See Christian de Chergé, *L'Invincible*, p. 96.
18. See Kiser, *Monks*, p. 75.

19: CONCLUSION: THE 'MONK WITHIN' AND UNIVERSAL SOLIDARITY

1. See Raimundo Panikkar, *Blessed Simplicity: The Monk as Universal Archetype* (New York: Seabury Press, 1982), pp. 11, 14, 15.

SUGGESTED FURTHER READING

(Please note that many of the best sources for the topics of monastic solitude and silence will be found in French or Italian only. I have referenced several of these sources in the endnotes.)

Allchin, A. M. (ed.), *Solitude and Communion: Papers on the Hermit Life* (Oxford: SLG Press, 1977).

Anon., *The Wound of Love: A Carthusian Miscellany* (Kalamazoo MI: Cistercian Publications, 1994).

Anon., *They Speak by Silences* (New York: David McKay, 1955).

Belisle, Augustin, *Into the Heart of God: Spiritual Reflections* (Petersham: St Bede's, 1989).

Belisle, Peter-Damian (ed.), *The Privilege of Love: Camaldolese Benedictine Spirituality* (Collegeville MN: Liturgical Press, 2002).

Colegate, Isabel, *A Pelican in the Wilderness: Hermits and Solitaries* (Washington DC: Counterpoint, 2002).

Fischer, Duncan, 'Liminality: The Vocation of the Church', *CSQ* 24 (1989), 181–205; *CSQ 25* (1990), 188–218.

France, Peter, *Hermits: The Insights of Solitude* (New York: St Martin's, 1996).

Funk, Mary Margaret, *Thoughts Matter: The Practice of Spiritual Life* (New York: Continuum, 1998).

Funk, Mary Margaret, *Tools Matter for Practicing the Spiritual Life* (New York: Continuum, 2002).

King, Margot H., *The Desert Mothers: A Survey of Feminine Anchoretic Tradition in Western Europe* (Saskatoon: Peregrina, 1984).

Leloir, Louis, 'The Message of the Desert Fathers: Then and Now', *American Benedictine Review* 40 (1989), 221–49.

The Lives of the Desert Fathers, tr. N. Russell (London: Mowbray, 1981).

Louf, André, *The Message of Monastic Spirituality* (New York: Desclée, 1964).

Merton, Thomas, *Contemplation in a World of Action* (Garden City NY: Doubleday, 1973).

Merton, Thomas, *Day of a Stranger* (Salt Lake City UT: Gibbs M. Smith, 1981).

Merton, Thomas, *Disputed Questions* (New York: Harcourt, 1953).

Merton, Thomas, *Love and Living* (New York: Harcourt, 1985).

Merton, Thomas, *The Monastic Journey* (Kalamazoo MI: Cistercian Publications, 1992).

Merton, Thomas, *Thoughts in Solitude* (New York: Farrar, Straus, Giroux, 1958).

A Monk, *The Hermitage Within: Spirituality of the Desert* (New York: Paulist Press, 1982).

Panikkar, Raimundo, *Blessed Simplicity: The Monk as Universal Archetype* (New York: Seabury Press, 1982).

Panikkar, Raimundo, 'The Contribution of Christian Monasticism in Asia to the Universal Church', *Cistercian Studies Quarterly* 10 (1975), 73–84.

Pinions (pseud.), *Wind on the Sand: The Story of a Twentieth-Century Anchoress* (New York: Paulist Press, 1981).

The Sayings of the Desert Fathers: The Alphabetical Collection, tr. B. Ward (Kalamazoo MI: Cistercian Publications, 1975).

Swann, Laura, *The Forgotten Desert Mothers: Sayings, Lives, and Stories of Early Christian Women* (New York: Paulist Press, 2001).

Ward, Benedicta, *Harlots of the Desert* (Kalamazoo MI: Cistercian Publications, 1982).

The Wisdom of the Desert Fathers: Apophthegmata Patrum from the Anonymous Series, tr. B. Ward (Oxford: SLG Press, 1975).

Word & Spirit 15 (1993). The entire issue's theme is the spiritual journey.

The World of the Desert Fathers: Stories and Sayings from the Anonymous Series of the Apophthegmata Patrum, tr. C. Stewart (Oxford: SLG Press, 1986).